For N

Blessings A

your Path —

Mark Thurston

Willing To Change: The Journey of Personal Transformation

Willing To Change: The Journey of Personal Transformation

Mark Thurston, Ph.D.

WE PUBLISH BOOKS
UNITED STATES OF AMERICA

We Publish Books
P.O. Box 1814
Rancho Mirage, CA 92270

www.WePublishBooks.com
E-mail: WePublishBooks@gmail.com

Library of Congress Cataloging in Publication Data:
Library of Congress Control Number: 2005910001

Thurston, Mark
Willing To Change: The Journey of Personal Transformation

Printed in the United States and London

Photograph by Michael Thurston
Cover designed by Rhonda Clifton Lyons

Willing To Change: The Journey of Personal Transformation
/ by Mark Thurston

BODY, MIND & SPIRIT / General / OCC000000
SELF-HELP / Personal Growth / General / SEL031000
PSYCHOLOGY / Applied Psychology / PSY003000

ISBN 10: 1-929841-26-4 Paperback
ISBN 13: 9781929841219 Paperback

ISBN 10: 1-929841-27-2 Hard Cover
ISBN 13: 9781929841271 Hard Cover

First Printing 2005

We Publish Books

Dedication

This book is dedicated to Rudolf E. Wilhelm, M.D. who for many years was my close friend and mentor. From the late 1970s until his death five years ago, Dr. Wilhelm was the man who most consistently and persistently challenged me to face my fears and undertake the long yet rewarding journey of personal transformation.

It was one of the joys of my life to co-found the Personal Transformation and Courage Institute with him and my wife Mary Elizabeth Lynch. It is an organization devoted to the very principles that are described in this book. I hope its readers will experience that same challenge to stretch themselves and discover the extraordinary resources of creativity and health and happiness that live inside us all.

Acknowledgments

The author wishes to acknowledge and thank the Rudolf E. Wilhelm Fund of the Community Foundation for Southeastern Michigan for its generous support in the research and writing of this book. This support has made it possible to synthesize the many extraordinary traditions of personal transformation, along with the personal experiences of students who have been part of the courses of the Personal Transformation and Courage Institute. Without the help of the Foundation, this book would not have been possible.

Thanks also go to individuals who have been my teachers and mentors for subjects related to personal transformation. Many of them I have known personally, but others I know only through their writings: Carl Jung, Lama Anagarika Govinda, G.I. Gurdjieff, P.D. Ouspensky, Maurice Nicoll, Edgar Cayce, Roberto Assagioli, Rudolf Steiner, William James, Bengt Stern, Jacob Needleman, Rudolf Wilhelm, and Osho.

This book also would not have been possible without the support of people who have helped me shape its ideas and prepare the manuscript: my wife, Mary Elizabeth Lynch, John Hishon, Denise Dahl, and Theresa Parente. And finally, a word of thanks to our son Michael, whose photograph taken on the Kepler Track, South Island of New Zealand, so wonderfully captures the spirit of this book.

Table of Contents

SUMMARY of CONTENTS

Part I: PERSONAL TRANSFORMATION & COURAGE

Chapter 1 THE SOUL'S JOURNEY: FOUR PHASES OF TRANSFORMATION

This chapter presents the fundamental image of the book: the symbolic journey of the soul that passes through four archetypal stages. The image is inspired by the spiritual philosopher Rudolf Steiner. These four Phases of transformation are:

- Catching the Vision – letting go of old values and plans, and committing oneself to a new image of what is possible in one's life – something new that can be clearly seen and experienced, even though it is still far off.
- The Difficult Journey – the uphill struggle to start trying to manifest the vision, a period of considerable effort and confrontation with obstacles, and a period when clear perception of the vision and ideal may be blocked from view.
- The Descent – just when progress seems to be made, there is a loss, death or failure. It may come as the meeting of one's own shadow self – but whatever form it takes, there is no longer the sense of climbing up toward the goal but of having fallen into the abyss.
- The Ally – at the depths of the Descent one finds self faced with something that looks insurmountable. Only the help of something bigger than oneself can redeem the situation, and yet it is no sure thing that one will even be willing to accept the help of the Ally when it comes into one's life.

This chapter will also explore a multi-faceted definition of "courage" and its role in the transformation process; it will also give a detailed description of what happens in one's life as he or she passes through each of the four Phases of a transformational journey. It will be noted for the reader that these Phases are cyclical and repeat themselves, just like the seasons of nature. For example, one is likely to have had several times of "Catching the Vision" and to have had repeated instances of "The Descent."

Chapter 2: CHALLENGES OF THE SECOND HALF OF LIFE

Soul transformation work, according to Jung and other depth psychologists, is truly the task of the second half of life. Up until the age of about 40, one is still wrestling primarily with issues related to ego-formation and trying to develop a healthy sense of one's personality self. But then something changes, and the challenges become deeper. Now the search for oneself as a soul can begin in earnest. This chapter examines models to help us understand these two sides of ourselves:

- The personality or egoic sense of self, and
- The individuality, essence or soul-self.

From those models there is an examination of what might have gone wrong in the first decades of one's life – experiences, which have to be "undone" or healed in order for soul transformation to take place in the second half of life.

Part II: MAPS AND METHODS FOR SOUL TRANSFORMATION

Chapter 3: THE TRANSFORMATION OF TIME

The human soul operates outside of the familiar constraints of linear time. And so the transformation of ourselves as souls requires a fundamental alteration in the way we relate to time and experience its control over us. This chapter explores the psychological and spiritual meaning of the astounding facts coming from modern physics research, especially quantum mechanics: Time is not what we think it is. Time is multi-dimensional, and we are not trapped in time the way our mechanistic, materialistic ways of thinking would conclude.

As we expand consciousness to discover that "all time is one time" -- that time is fluid and rhythmic and repetitive -- then we are open to powerful ways in which we can reconstruct our relationship to past events (making healing and forgiveness more accessible) and even have a conscious connection to the "future self," the person that already lives within us as potentialities.

Chapter 4: TRANSFORMATIVE MEDITATION

The ancient practice of meditation – rediscovered and renewed for 21st century men and women – is the single most important discipline for the transformation of the soul. This chapter takes the insights from the previous chapters and presents practical ways in which soul transformation can be enhanced by daily meditation. First, the chapter offers an easy-to-learn way to start meditating – an approach that is universal and does not require any specific religious beliefs. But meditation is described not just as a period of sitting with eyes closed and mind focused on a mantra. Meditation becomes, instead, an entire way of being and approaching life. In this way meditation truly is the most important element of the transformation process.

Part III: THE HUMAN WILL AS THE KEY TO SOUL TRANSFORMATION

Chapter 5: WHAT IS FREE WILL?

Along with mind and spirit, the will constitutes one of the three basic building blocks of our soul nature. The will is that which can make us free and independent. It gives us our sense of individuality. But paradoxically it is also the aspect of the soul that allows us to connect with the universal spirit. It is through a healthy will that courage most directly manifests in our lives.

In this chapter we will briefly explore the history of how philosophy, religion and psychology have understood free will. Then, a nine-point definition of will is presented, creating a more expansive and useful understanding than the narrow-minded notion of "willpower" that is common today. Those nine-points are: active principle, individualizer, chooser, agent of obedience, changer, opposer of mind, developer, motivator, and guide.

Chapter 6: THE SEVEN QUALITIES OF THE WILL

Seven distinct qualities of the will were first proposed by Dr. Roberto Assagioli (the founder of Psychosynthesis), who observed them in his clinical practice of transpersonal psychotherapy. In contrast to the nine-part definition of will which remains more abstract and theoretical, these seven qualities concern how free will actually manifests in daily living – i.e., the faces it shows to us. They are essential to the path of soul transformation. And as we work consciously to nurture and develop each one of them, a healthy will begins to emerge – a will that can support and express the courageous spirit of the soul. The seven qualities are:

- Vitality
- Self-discipline and control
- Courageous initiative
- Patient persistence
- Decisiveness
- Focus and concentration
- Synthesis and harmony

This chapter builds upon the original insights of Assagioli, adding a discussion of how certain "bogus" qualities try to pose as authentic free will but are actually distortions and caricatures of the genuine attribute. For example, "repression" standing in place of "self-discipline," or "obsession" acting as a false substitute for "focus and concentration."

Chapter 7: STAGES IN DEVELOPING YOUR WILL

This chapter presents another new model of the human will and how it can be used for soul transformation. It starts with a model describing how mind and will interact to create human consciousness, and how a more healthy will gives the power to heal and transform the patterns that are stored in the human soul. In fact, to be successful with the transformational path of the soul, it demands that we not be afraid of our own power. This chapter presents a five-step model for how we reclaim the authentic power of the soul – a model that has stages numbered zero through four:

0) *The Sleeping Will.* We are "asleep" to the faculties of soul and

just reacting habitually to what life throws at us. It is labeled "zero" because we are lacking any genuine power or connection with the soul-self. In this section we will examine the ways that we "leak" power in our daily experiences, especially when we lack the courage to meet life directly and honestly.

1) *Negating Will.* We express the courage to set limits and define ourselves with a "No." The assertion of our boundaries is a starting point in reclaiming our soul power.
2) *Skillful Will.* We develop the courage and wisdom to know how and when to say "Yes" to aspects of life, in addition to the skill of knowing how and when to stick with a "No." But even at this stage of reclaiming our power, we are still in primarily a responsive and reacting stance toward life.
3) *Empowering Will.* At this stage we go beyond just reacting and responding to life courageously and wisely. Now we discover our power to actually shape our life circumstances and to be fully creative with a strong and healthy sense of personal empowerment.
4) *Transpersonal Will.* Here we go beyond our own personal empowerment, but it requires the courage to surrender and let go. Only then can a higher power work through us, a power that comes from the connection that exists between the soul and the universal spirit.

Chapter 8: METHODS OF AWAKENING YOUR WILL

This final chapter is highly practical. Even when readers realize just how important the will truly is – still they are left with the practical question, "How can I awaken and develop my will?" Just as surely as there are exercises to train aspects of the mind, so too there are will development methods. This chapter describes a series of such methods, and it invites the reader to undertake a will development program for him or herself. And with the will seen as the key to any authentic soul development work, this highly pragmatic chapter is a fitting chapter with which to conclude.

Part I:

PERSONAL TRANSFORMATION AND COURAGE

Chapter 1

The Soul's Journey: Four Phases of Transformation

Change is the one constant in modern life. Nothing seems to stand still anymore – especially in the dizzying flux of the *outside* world. To find some personal stability it's only natural to want to hang on to who you are *inwardly* – to figure out who you are and then stick with it. That's the appeal of fundamentalism in the 21st century – whether it means religious, scientific, or personal fundamentalism: getting hold of a truth and then hanging onto it for dear life.

Sadly, that approach isn't very likely to bring happiness or peace of mind. If you become inwardly set in your ways, then the outside winds of change will buffet you and pull you apart. To live harmoniously in a world that's always changing requires inner flexibility. Your inner life needs to be just as dynamic as the outer world in which you live.

It all comes down to your *willingness to change*. Are you ready to see your life as a never-ending adventure to become more aware? Are you willing to continually let go of old beliefs and understandings and never settle in to any rigid, final view of what your life is all about or who you are?

"Willingness" itself is a fascinating word. It stands as the mirror opposite to "willfulness" – that demanding, pushy approach to life that is celebrated in the media and foisted on us as the only way to survive in a competitive, self-centered world. To many people, "willingness" just sounds too weak or passive – too much like allowing someone else to control your life. But if we explore the nature of "willingness" a little more deeply, we discover that it's the essence of transformation. Its openness creates the climate for inner development and maturity. Its capacity for trust and surrender makes it possible for powerful forces to work through us.

Two Kinds of Change

When we consider the meaning of personal change, it's important to distinguish between improvement and transformation, two terms that are often misleadingly used as synonyms. Both involve change, but one is more radical and ultimately much more significant than the other.

Improvement – or self-improvement – involves creating a better version of essentially the same person. It's a matter of polishing up what we'll call in this book the personality self – the familiar persona that we generally know ourselves to be and that we show to the world. All that is well and good. Self-improvement is a worthy endeavor, but we shouldn't kid ourselves into thinking that it results in reaching our potentials.

Transformation, on the other hand, is a quantum jump in our sense of self. It's the awakening of what we will call the individuality self – the soul essence of who we are. Both sides of us are important, but make no mistake about which is more important.

Transformation is a more challenging kind of change process because the personality self doesn't easily surrender its claim to be the whole of who we are. But unless we are willing to undergo an authentic transformation, something in the soul remains restless and unfulfilled.

Transformative change usually brings three ingredients into your life – three elements that help you connect to your extraordinary potential for creativity, joy, and purposeful service in the world.

Transformation brings more light into your life – more awareness. Light and illumination (as soul awakening is sometimes called) brings new capacity to see what's going on inside and outside of you. And light brings vibrancy and vitality – sure signposts that a genuine transformation is taking place.

Transformation gives you greater access to power – your own power. In other words, when you go through the quantum jump of a personal transformation – one in which the individuality self is significantly roused – then you gain access to a new kind of power in your life. And certainly with that enhanced power comes greater responsibility.

Transformation brings into your life more spirituality than

materiality. The quality most frequently associated with spirituality is oneness; whereas materiality relates to life as distinctions, differences, competition, and opposites. And so, with authentic transformation *you begin to respond to life in terms of its wholeness and its unity.*

A Hint from Science about the Nature of Transformation

Physical science gives us an important lesson about what to expect from transformative change. It's a reminder that sometimes there are important transformative forces at work, even when results are not quick to show up. The lesson comes from how a substance like water undergoes a transformation from one state to another. For example, think about what's required to turn liquid water into steam. They are chemically identical: H_2O. However, water has three possible states (ice, liquid water, and steam), and much is required to move from one state into another.

Consider what's needed to heat ice-cold water at 32 degrees Fahrenheit up to the point where it turns into steam. We can measure this scientifically, and a remarkable fact emerges. Calories are units of energy, and it takes 100 calories to heat a gram of water from ice-cold right up to the point where it reaches 212 degrees Fahrenheit. But then we have to pump in another 540 calories of energy – that is, more than five times the amount we have already invested – in order to get the water to transform from scalding hot liquid at 212 into steam, still at that same 212 degrees. That extra investment of energy is called "latent heat." It's invisible, in a sense, because there doesn't seem to be any tangible result while that extra energy is going in. While those 540 calories of energy are going in, the scalding hot water looks like it remains just scalding hot water, still at 212 degrees. However, something very significant is happening at a molecular level. Preparation for a dramatic transformation – a change of state – is taking place.

Consider that personal transformation often works in the same way. Once you are willing to change, once you are committed to transformational change in your life, you may find that considerable effort, attention, and time is required before it looks like things have altered in your life. But something important is going on during that altered in your life. But something important is going on during that "latency period." The energy is being invested in a way that can ultimately lead to a change in the state of who you are. It's worth the patient and consistent efforts required.

Courage and the Phases of Transformation

A willingness to change means entering into a process that has *rhythm* and *pattern*. Certainly there will be times when things seem chaotic – even out of control. Often it's only in hindsight that you'll be able to see that the forces of transformative change have led you through purposeful stages – one building upon the next. Knowing a little bit *in advance* about these stages can be reassuring, especially if you are about to make a commitment to cooperate with the winds of change.

In this first chapter we'll start by exploring a four-fold pattern of transformative change. It would be nice if you had to pass through these stages only once in life. They describe a very challenging progression – one that requires considerable courage – and most of us would prefer to have to do this only once. But life isn't structured that way, any more than nature requires only one wintertime. No, like the seasons of nature, the four stages of transformational change are a cycle. And with each completion of the sequence, we grow stronger and closer to what we are destined for in this life.

Let's look at the qualities of these four Phases of the transformational journey. A powerful image to capture this adventurous journey of personal transformation can be seen in a crayon drawing made by Dr. Rudolf Steiner, an Austrian spiritual philosopher of the late 19th and early 20th century. In this artwork Steiner emblematically depicts the journey of the soul. The individual in the drawing must traverse a difficult pathway over treacherous, hilly terrain. The path has four Phases to it, and each Phase requires a kind of courage. Here is a contemporary artist's rendition of the themes in Steiner's original crayon creation.

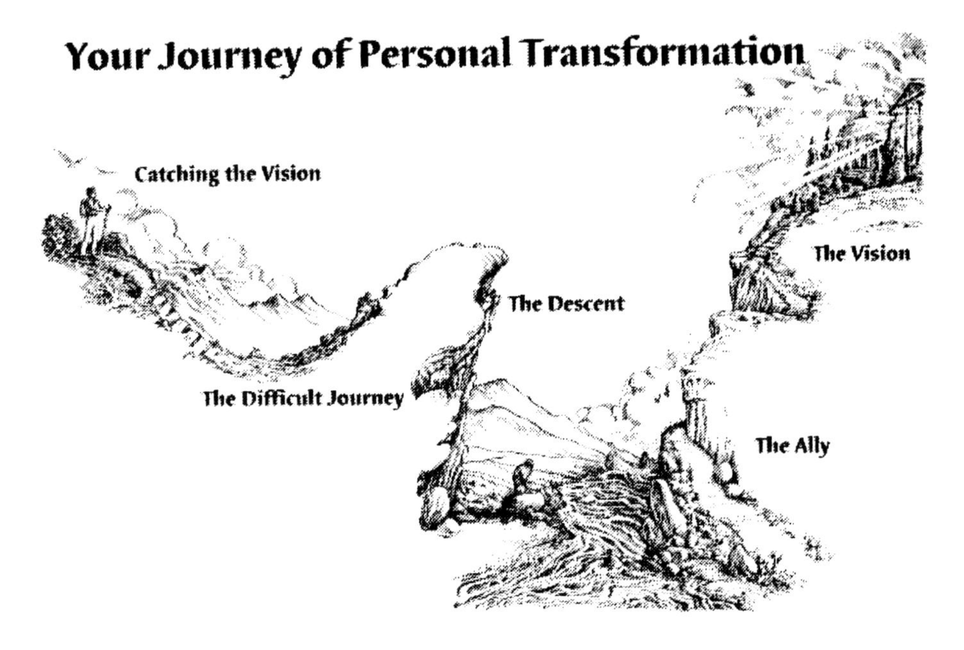

One-by-one let's examine the characteristics and the challenges of these Phases. They are a universal pattern, but they usually have a unique way in which they play out in our lives. For example, the way in which one person encounters Phase 3 – the Descent – is likely to be very different than the way it happens to someone else. What's more, within one individual's life story there are likely to be variations. A Phase 3 experience in one's mid-thirties might be very different than a Phase 3 experience in the mid-fifties. For now, just try to get an overall sense of the nature of each step; then you can look back at your own life story for evidence of these Phases, as well as seeing what Phase you seem to be in right now along your journey of personal transformation.

1. Catching the Vision.

First, the traveler – the soul on its journey – comes to a place where she can see far into the distance, even catching the glimpse of a sacred temple on a far-off peak. This distant vision symbolizes the shaping of one's ideal, the active creation of one's purpose for the coming years. This requires a special kind of courage. Simply to shape an ideal demands the brave willingness to let go of limited, out-grown values and plans. We all know how hard it is to let go of old, familiar values and stretch ourselves by adopting a new vision.

There are rare times in our lives when we catch such a glimpse of possibilities. What special moments they are. In an instant a spell is broken and we see with fresh eyes. In an instant, the hypnotic trance is shattered – a trance that has kept us stuck in familiar, routine ways of seeing ourselves. Suddenly we see clearly for a moment. We see beyond just today and this week, and a much broader and more promising future appears. It's the moment of being a visionary.

But how many of us think of ourselves as visionaries? It sounds rather presumptuous. Visionaries are surely great religious figures, or perhaps great pioneers in their field, such as medicine or the arts. It even sounds a little audacious to consider yourself a visionary – to put yourself on the same level as great men and women of the past.

And yet, we are all visionaries, probably multiple times in our lives. It's safe to say that most all of us have times in life when we are inspired by the clear perception of what we could become. The possibilities aren't just abstract either. We can feel and even "taste" what it would be like to become something more than we have been – especially "something more" in regard to our talents and abilities.

When has that happened for you? Most likely, there was a time like this in late adolescence or in early adulthood. A period of idealism – not just imagining a more ideal world in which to live, but also catching the vision of the role that you could play in that world. Such idealism probably had something to do with dropping the worldview and values of your parents and peers. It meant staking a claim to your own image of life's purposefulness. And that may have taken considerable courage. The inner and outer voices that steer our lives don't easily surrender their power. There is a struggle to be a visionary, and sometimes that struggle is most vigorous in freeing ourselves from the inner voices that insist that we stay with what is familiar.

But surely age eighteen or twenty-two wasn't the only time in your life that you've experienced "Catching the Vision." Perhaps in your late twenties or early thirties it came again. After some measure of accomplishment (even success, perhaps) with your career or having children or exploring different places to live, *something in you began to feel the need for change – that there had to be something more.* You were hungry for a new vision to inspire you. Once again that would take courage because it would mean letting go of much that was familiar. Once again you were required to follow your own internal compass and not settle for someone else's opinion.

And so life progresses. From one inspired vision to the next. But is this a progression that produces growth and transformation? Or is it just a string of fantasies along which you bounce? It all depends upon what goes on in those months and years that lie between the visionary moments. Transformation is by no means guaranteed. Just because you catch a vision of the person you could become doesn't mean you ever take even the first step toward realizing it.

In fact, don't we all know people who seem to have lived a life that is merely one visionary dream after another? Every few years there is yet another exciting possibility, but nothing ever seems to come of any of them. The problem is that the individual is not following through on the other three phases of the transformative journey.

2. The Difficult Journey

Next along this challenging pathway, the traveler comes to rugged terrain, with many obstacles and many ups and downs. Often along this part of the journey, the far-off goal is blocked from view, and the sacred temple is no longer in sight. Once again courage is crucial. When we temporarily lose sight of our aspiration – when the vision of what we are after gets fogged or blocked – it requires a special kind of courage to "keep on keeping on."

This Phase of the transformative process requires focused effort. Once there is a clear vision, then the work of manifestation begins. It's the purposeful work – inwardly on yourself and outwardly in the world – to express the vision you've seen. And that usually feels like an uphill struggle. There are various boulders and obstacles along the way – each one demanding skillful negotiation. Often it's only through faith that you continue trying. You have to keep remembering, "Yes, I have seen something in the distance that *is real*. Even though I cannot see it right now, I know it's there and worth striving for."

3. The Descent

Here's the part of the journey we all wish to avoid. It's the scariest because it feels like the bottom is dropping out of our world. The traveler now faces the biggest challenge yet. Just when progress was being made, it suddenly feels like all the gains are lost. In Steiner's drawing the pathway descends sharply. There can be no further approach to the sacred place on the hill unless there's first a descent. In what appears to be almost a precipitous drop, the road goes steeply and treacherously downward.

The Descent symbolizes those points in our lives when we must be brave and go into the depths of the soul, especially to encounter what is called in Jungian psychology the "shadow self" – our fears and the rejected sides of ourselves. What courage that demands!

How might we experience this Phase? Sometimes it is the loss of one's job or the death of a loved one. It could be a personal breakdown – physically, mentally, or spiritually. Or the Descent may come as a long-avoided confrontation with one's own arrogance, greed, mean-spiritedness, shame, or depression. This is the "dark night of the soul" but it's a necessary part of the transformative journey.

4. The Ally

In the depths of this canyon, the traveler faces a final obstacle – one that seems insurmountable. A body of water looms before him. There is no bridge, and at first the waters look to be uncrossable. How frustrating because just across this body of water is the final ascent that leads to the sacred temple on the mountaintop. With a kind of divine grace, there's a small boat and boatsman at hand to ferry the traveler across, but only if he will trust and accept this assistance.

These are the moments we long for, the times when help comes even in the face of a daunting problem. That Ally can symbolize a resource that comes from within yourself – a strength or talent that emerges unexpectedly to meet the crisis. It can come as a teaching or a mentor. It can be a therapist or a friend.

But we don't automatically accept the offer of help from the Ally. It can take considerable courage to climb aboard that boat, to accept the assistance. And why is that so hard? Simply because something in us realizes that we'll never be the same once we cross over into the land of our vision and ideal. It's clearly a risk to accept the help.

Of course, even upon successfully reaching the sacred place – the ideal – the journey isn't over. The cycle merely starts all over again. Having reached the mountaintop and the sacred place, it's then possible to see off into the distance once again. A new vision can come clearly into view. And like the seasons of nature, the sequence of transformation starts again.

But this is not going in circles. Instead, it is like a spiral, and each cycle through these four Phases of transformation is like one turn on the spiral that in itself has a direction. When we can relax into this cyclical rhythm of our lives, a special quality of patience can begin to emerge. Like the biblical writer of Ecclesiastes, we can realize, "There is a time for everything, and a season for every activity under heaven." (3:1-3) We can begin to appreciate the value and the challenges inherent in each of the four Phases of this courageous journey to experience transformational change.

A Deeper Look at Courage

Courage is crucial to personal change, but it's so easily misunderstood. We're given superficial, sensationalistic images of courage by the modern media. It's depicted as a kind of daredevil recklessness, and we're asked to believe that courage is superhuman bravado stemming from fearlessness.

But what a caricature! Instead of buying into such an unrealistic distortion of this vital quality, we need to look deeper and find its true meaning. Courage is a multifaceted talent of the soul that is indispensable to personal transformation. Consider these six points about courage – principles that redefine what this special quality is really all about. Your capacity to genuinely change depends on cultivating this kind of authentic courage.

Courage activates your ideal. Two elements have to be present in your life in order to change: vision and courage. Having the first without the second is sure to lead to a life of frustration and disappointment. A piece of wisdom from the spiritual philosophy of Edgar Cayce hits the nail right on the head: "He without an ideal is sorry indeed; he with an ideal and lacking courage to live it is sorrier still. Know that." (1402-1)

No doubt we're all guilty from time to time of such a "sorry" state, of catching a lofty vision but then not living it courageously. This sort of failing seems to be an unavoidable part of being human. But maybe it really *is* possible to muster this invaluable fruit of the spirit – courage – and have it propel us along the spiritual path of transformation.

Courage is living from the heart. The word "courage" comes from the root word "cor" which means "heart." In our very language there is an understanding that courage comes not from the intellect or muscle power. Courage arises from intuition and the soul.

As the mystic and meditation teacher Osho has pointed out, there is a fundamental difference in the way that the head and the heart operate. The head is a businessman – it is calculating and cunning. In contrast, the heart is a gambler and willing to move into the unknown. The heart knows that life is not a problem to be solved; it's a mystery to be explored.

Courage means taking risks in life. How do you see your life – as a search for security or as a call to adventure? There may be many voices in your mind cautioning you to play it safe. Whether that conditioning comes from your parents or the society around you, it's the compulsion to play it safe and not be courageous.

Taking risks means that mistakes will surely be made along the way. It means that sometimes you will discover you've gone the wrong way, and there's a price to be paid for the errors. But those aren't mistakes that have to happen again, and you can learn deeply from them.

Risk-taking doesn't mean recklessness. There's nothing inherently self-defeating in risk-tasking – in fact, it's life-affirming because you state boldly that you're not going to settle for what is safe and familiar yet essentially a life that's dead. Instead, courageous risk-taking can be something as simple as not having a plan all the time. It can mean living today with spontaneity. Or, it can mean believing in yourself and your talents, even if others think you are sure to fail in the cynical, competitive world.

Courage means moving ahead with life in spite of fears. We often have the distorted idea that courage comes only when we have dispelled all of our fears. That sounds like a nearly impossible task, and so who would ever get around to being courageous? Aren't we all doomed to be cowards?

There is little difference, however, between a coward and a courageous person. Both have fears. The coward listens to the fears and follows their advice; whereas, the courageous man or woman moves ahead with life *in spite of* those fears.

Courage is living with uncertainty. The careful, calculating side of us wants guarantees before moving ahead with life. That voice in us says, "I'm willing to change but only if the results are certain." A pre-condition like that virtually assures that no change will happen. Life can never guarantee results, and so we stick with the status quo.

In contrast, courage allows us to step into the vacuum of uncertainty. The courageous voice in us says, "There's no guarantees, but it's worth the risk." That kind of courage allows us to be patient, and it gives us the strength to deal with ambiguity.

Courage means facing that which troubles and disturbs you. To go on a journey of personal transformation is sure to stir up memories and patterns that will be upsetting. Because that sounds like something unhappy or distasteful, you're likely to avoid making changes in your life. Who wants to have to confront troubling, disturbing feelings that arise?

But the psychological fact of the matter is that whenever you go on a genuine inner quest to know yourself better and to experience transformative change, then you are sure to have times of feeling bad. This principle is found in one of the sayings of Jesus from the Gnostic *Gospel of Thomas*, discovered by biblical archaeologists in the late 1940s: "Those who seek should not stop seeking until they find. When they find, they will be disturbed. When they are disturbed, they will marvel, and will reign over all." The self-mastery that is promised at the end of this sequence is not something you can directly jump to. First, you must be well motivated to make the quest. And then, once you find the object of your quest, you should expect to discover in it something that will "disturb you" – some translations say "trouble." It's courage that allows you to face that which is troubling or disturbing. Courage makes it possible to face the dark sides of life – one's shadow self – and continue the transformative journey.

In summary, the journey of personal transformation is essentially one of courage. Each step along the pathway demands this vital quality of the human soul. Especially in the second half of life we face important questions about our willingness to change, and courage will be among the most important ingredients to make that possible. In Chapter 2 we'll examine more closely the two sides of ourselves – the personality and the individuality – and we'll explore the patterns with which we must struggle in order to courageously awaken to who we really are.

Chapter 2

Challenges of the Second Half of Life

Transformational change, according to Carl Jung and other depth psychologists, is truly the task of the second half of life. Up until the age of about forty, one is still wrestling primarily with issues related to ego-formation and trying to develop a healthy personality. But then something changes, and the challenges become deeper. Now the search for oneself as a soul can begin in earnest – *if one is willing to change*.

Everything about transformational change depends on being able to distinguish between two sides of ourselves:

- The personality or egoic sense of self, and
- The individuality, essence or soul-self.

In this chapter we'll explore what might have gone wrong in the first decades of one's life as the personality was taking shape – problems which have to be "undone" or healed in order for soul transformation to take place in the second half of life. If one is truly *willing* to make these kinds of changes, then supportive disciplines and methods can be powerful ways to initiate the process, and we'll examine some of them at the end of the chapter.

Personality and Individuality

When we honestly and sincerely follow a balanced approach to self-study, we are likely to make an important discovery. Each person fundamentally is made up of two parts: personality and individuality. Personality is the mask that you wear in daily life. It's the way you appear to others, and it includes your mannerisms, your likes, and dislikes. Personality is the product of imitation. From the moment you were born and began to observe the world around you, personality began to take shape. You learned from your parents, television, and teachers, just to name a few of the most likely influences. This is called *conditioning*.

Over time your personality took on a particular set of qualities that are unique to you. However one characteristic of personality is the same for everyone: the habitual, involuntary way in which it operates. Personality runs on automatic pilot; it reacts to life situations in very predictable ways. For example, think of someone you know very well, perhaps a spouse or child. You can probably imagine a specific kind of problem situation for which you are sure you know how that person will react. You've seen the habitual attitudes, emotions, or behaviors so often in that sort of circumstance that you are positive it would happen the same way again. And, so long as that person is operating from the level of his or her personality, you're right – the routine response is predictable.

Personality is not inherently good or bad. Some of the strong habit patterns we have developed are nice, and others aren't so nice. What characterizes personality is the way it operates rather unconsciously.

This idea is carefully described in the writings of P. D. Ouspensky, a Russian teacher of consciousness transformation. Ouspensky wrote about the automatic, mechanical personality in his autobiography, *In Search of the Miraculous* (an account of his studies under G. I. Gurdjieff). Both Gurdjieff and Ouspensky taught that humanity in its normal waking consciousness is in a kind of sleep state relative to genuine spiritual consciousness. In other words, we move through physical life sixteen or eighteen hours a day erroneously believing that we are self-conscious beings. We imagine that we frequently make free-willed choices; but the truth of the matter is just the opposite. We usually operate as a personality self and merely react unconsciously to the demands of life. Any efforts to change – as long as we are operating just from personality – are bound to be short-lived and rather futile.

Perhaps the theory of Gurdjieff and Ouspensky sounds discouraging. But watch someone carefully; or better yet, watch yourself. What you're likely to see is how readily you fall into automatic routines. You'll find that you think the same old thoughts, replay the accustomed emotional patterns, spout the same familiar words, and move with consistent mannerisms. Recognizing this can even be humorous, although laughter comes more quickly when it's someone else's mechanicalness and not your own that's pointed out.

Sometimes our habits are so strong we virtually become caricatures of ourselves. A favorite technique of comedians is impersonation. Audiences howl with delight to see the personality traits of a famous person imitated. Sometimes the joke comes from exaggerating an obvious fault in that well-known individual; but maybe there is another side to our amusement. Could we be laughing at ourselves, too? Maybe something in us wakes up for just a moment when we clearly see the typical human condition.

These descriptions of the personality make it sound at best worthless and at worst an unavoidable obstacle to personal transformation. However, it's probably necessary to have a personality to function in the world, simply because we need to be able to do certain things automatically. Driving a car, washing the dishes, or tying your shoes would be laborious if you had to make every movement with full consciousness.

As already mentioned, the personality side of our being isn't necessarily bad or wrong; it has an important role to play if it is used properly. The key to using it properly is getting in touch with our individuality. This forgotten part of ourselves is our spiritual core. Many labels can be used – Higher Self, Real I, or Higher Ego – but the word individuality nicely captures its essence. To get a better feeling for this side of ourselves, let's look at five of its qualities. They're simple to remember because each one ends with the letters i-t-y: unity, continuity, sensitivity, creativity, and activity.

The individuality of the soul bestows a profound sense of uniqueness, but paradoxically it is also in touch with the oneness of all life – its *unity*. The individuality is conscious of the unity of all creation. It directly experiences its connections with God, other souls, and the natural environment.

The individuality has *continuity* and permanence. Think about how you are in many ways a different person from who you were fifteen years ago, or fifteen years before that. And yet, in the midst of all that change, something has stayed the same. Despite all the identities that have come and gone, there is a thread of continuity. It's a dynamic continuity because *even the soul is in the process of development and growth* (a key point to keep in mind). For those willing to entertain the possibility of reincarnation from one human life to the next human life, the personality dissolves soon after death, but it's the individuality that lives on and is capable of transformation.

The individuality has *sensitivity* not just to physical influences but to the non-material realm as well. It has innate intuitive abilities and can perceive things from invisible, spiritual dimensions. This natural psychic gift often operates quietly, almost behind the scenes by gently guiding us with hunches and feelings. It presents us with a special kind of wisdom: knowing something without being able to explain how we know it.

The individuality has *creativity*. Whereas the personality is caught up in routine and habit, the individuality is original and inventive. It sees life with fresh eyes and creates new responses to old difficulties. It is imaginative and able to perceive novel approaches to life. Inspired individuality brings the qualities of the infinite down into individual, finite expression.

Finally, the individuality displays *activity*. This level of one's being is not passive or hidden. Every day it is involved in life, even though the personality self may ignore its presence. The individuality constantly takes the initiative to influence conscious awareness and to provide helpful support for spiritual growth. The personality self may not want to change and may resist these overtures, but it doesn't deter the active, involved individuality self.

Do these five qualities sound familiar? Are you in touch with the individuality side of yourself from time to time? One good way to clarify your personal awareness of the Higher Self is to think about the very best in yourself. Take a moment to remember instances that reflected your own excellence. They are times when you were functioning at the optimum. Don't be concerned with how frequently you have been in touch with this side of yourself; just re-experience the reality of your "individuality identity."

The Human Personality as a Wheel

A visual image may help you get a clearer sense of what is meant by the personality. Consider the metaphor of a wheel. If you are on the rim of a rotating wheel, you get the feeling of movement toward a goal, but in the end the wheel merely brings you back to the point from which you began. In the same fashion, your personality may often appear to lead you in new directions only to bring you back to the same issues or problems in life.

To help illustrate this further, think of a time in your life when you wanted to make a change in order to get away from a troublesome person or condition. Perhaps it was a situation in which you could not see your own role in the creation of the problem and tended to blame others, so you wanted out. Perhaps your example relates to a job or a close personal relationship.

Did the change actually solve the problem? Most likely you experienced temporary relief from the difficulty, only to discover months or years later that the same kind of issue or problem was arising again in the new situation, job, or relationship. Because something in you had not been changed, you were drawn back to a similar difficulty. Because your habitual personality was responsible, at least in part, for the creation of the original problem, it was again involved in the creation of the repeated difficulty. *Whenever your personality is controlling your behavior, there will be a strong tendency to repeat the past.* In this sense we can say that your personality is like a rotating wheel: It appears to move in a direction away from an old situation, only to bring you back later to the same point from which you began.

In the analogy of the wheel, many subpersonalities live on the rim. Each of these subpersonalities creates a particular feeling of personal identity. In the course of day, your attention moves from one to the next in rather random order.

What governs the shift from one sense of identity to the next are the events of daily living: what people say to you, what happens to the stock market, the weather, etc. We could think of these influences that arise from outer, material life as being like pushes which keep the wheel turning. You may recall the experience of helping a child enjoy a merry-go-round on a playground. With the child seated on the merry-go-round and you standing alongside it, you would have to give the rim of the merry-go-round a brief shove every five or ten seconds to keep it turning. Material life gives you those pushes. They prod you from one feeling of who you are to another and, in so doing, keep your wheel turning.

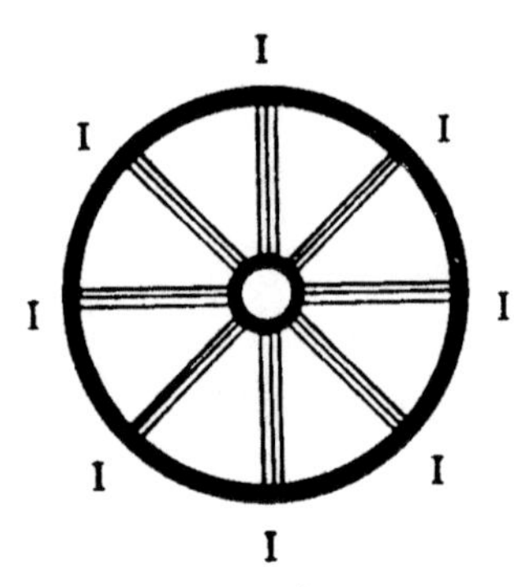

The subpersonalities are represented by the various "I's" on the rim of the wheel. Each "I" has associated with it a set of spokes. These spokes represent habitual traits which are a part of that particular "I" and its way of seeing and responding to the world. For example, if one of your subpersonalities could be labeled "the compulsive pleaser," you might find that certain attitudes, emotions, and behaviors manifest in an automatic, mechanical way whenever that subpersonality has your attention. The spokes might be labeled with words like "inferiority feelings" or "volunteers for tasks I don't have time to do" or "smiles a lot although it's not sincere," and so forth. Or, if another of your subpersonalities was labeled "the get-it-done administrator," the spokes might have labels like "feeling hurried" or "talks brusquely to subordinates" or "logically categorizes each experience."

Transformative change involves, most fundamentally, dis-identifying with the wheel of personality. It means awakening to another sense of oneself – the individuality – and allowing that deeper and more authentic state of being to start controlling the direction of your life.

A Closer Look at How the Personality Forms

The process of soul transformation is best understood by starting with the kinds of wounds, limitations and conditioning that we have undergone early in life. In essence, all of us had a difficult childhood. No matter how nice our parents may have been, there are unavoidable traumas that come with being a child. It starts with the horrific experience of physical birth and it continues with childhood upbringing. None of us escapes conditioning – none of us gets through childhood without having to betray our feelings. The formation of the personality self is sure to have included these difficult challenges.

These simple facts of childhood are not an invitation to a pity party. It's just a psychological fact of life, just as surely as there are physiological facts of life, such as baby teeth falling out or hair turning grey in old age. There are certain psychological effects that are bound to have happened to all of us in childhood. Clearly some people are much more wounded and conditioned than are others. But all of us carry limitations and handicaps from the birth experience and from childhood.

Of course, it might take many volumes and many experts to document all the factors involved in childhood wounding. And, admittedly, it's easy to get lost in the overwhelming array of experiences that might have happened to us. But surely there is a middle ground between these two extremes:

- Refusing to look at the past and assuming that what happened years ago is not really so influential – especially if we will just have enough willpower to push on into the future.
- Getting paralyzed by the memories of all the traumatic, wounding events of childhood – so paralyzed that no healthy future seems possible.

That middle ground is a willingness to go back and remember the past to experience the feelings and needs of the child that you were years ago. It means honoring that child and beginning to take responsibility for taking care *right now* of those needs and wounds. Your capacity to change is in large part dependent on this principle: *The child is still alive within you* – the unmet needs, the wounds, and the conditioning are still alive and active. The good news is that as a grown-up adult now, you can begin to "parent" that child and transform those handicaps. This is a crucial point: *you can "parent" yourself* – you can start right now providing yourself the quality of attention, self-love, and support that you have always needed. That can go a long way toward healing some of these wounds and traumas that self-exploration will unearth.

Let's consider just four types of experiences that you have gone through in one way or another as a child. Again, this consideration is not to make you feel sorry for yourself or to give you excuses for being the way you are now. But any hope for transformative change in your life depends on the courage to go back and recognize the foundation on which your personality self exists.

The trauma of birth. As one wisdom tradition puts it, "Dying is easy; being born is the hard part." The conditions of birth, experienced from the perspective of the child, are horrific. From an idyllic state, suddenly the child is subjected to terrifying pressure. It is an expulsion from Eden all over again, but this time it is an ordeal in which the child must struggle for his or her life. In some cases, the labor can go on for twenty-four hours or more. Just think how tired we get as adults doing strenuous physical activity for fifteen or twenty minutes. The infant must do something even more demanding for hour after hour. It may well be the most arduous endeavor one ever makes in life.

We might well wonder, then, if those delivered by Caesarean section have an easier time of it. Even though there is not the long struggle down the birth canal, there is a different kind of terror in being ripped from a place of perfect warmth and security. The psychological impact is likely to be very similar.

The point here is not just the extraordinary effort and terrifying struggle one must make. Equally significant is that each of us is imprinted with the memory of what it is like to be fully taken care of – to be in a place of comfort and security, to have one's needs being taken care of. Something in us remembers that this is possible. In many ways the in utero experience is the apex of life for us – our glimpse of heaven in materiality. And we may well live out our lives trying to find someone to make that happen for us all over again; but it's an impossible quest and sure to create only frustration and poisoned relationships.

What's more, we also remember at a subconscious level how scary it was to be taken from that perfect place. The trauma of birth can make us very reluctant to undertake any kind of transformative process that even hints that it may involve a similar ordeal.

Messages that you are not okay. The forces of socialization are unrelenting. No matter how much you may have been a "wanted child," you were sure to encounter in your early years a wide variety of messages that it's not safe to be yourself. This is not to say that parents ought to let the child run free with every desire and whim – that somehow this would make the emergence of the personality more healthy. Obviously, the child needs direction, both to protect the child from harm and to allow the child to function as part of a family and later as part of the community.

However, our upbringing almost invariably includes a lot more than just learning personal safety and good hygiene. *You were raised by adults who were not psychologically healthy themselves*; and even if you were an adored and wanted child, there were messages to you that certain impulses and innate desires on your part were not okay. Perhaps you had a natural curiosity that led you to wander away and upset your mother. Maybe you had a love for animals but having pets was out of the question for your family. Perhaps you had a fiery temperament but any expression of anger was upsetting to your father and you quickly got the message that this part of you was not acceptable.

Sexuality is another aspect of ourselves that often gets labeled as unacceptable. Modern psychology knows that even when we are very young there is an innate interest in sexuality. But parents, teachers, and childcare workers are usually adults who are not especially integrated with their own sexuality, and they are sure to pass their wounded understanding on to the child. In most societies in the Western world, the child learns early on that there is something not quite right about the body itself – whether its urination or bowel movements or sexual urges. To varying degrees we are taught, often very subtly, that the body is not really a friend and it cannot be trusted.

Trade-offs for getting love. The child just wants to be loved. It has come from a nine-month period of being perfectly loved and taken care of in that dark, warm, fluid-filled world inside mother. And quite naturally the child just wants to find support and love in the scary new world into which it has emerged.

But now there are rules and conditions. Love isn't so automatic, and as a child you had to learn exactly what was required of you in order to get what you craved. There would have to be trade-offs that involved giving up something of yourself in order to get the love you deeply needed. Sadly, this usually meant a certain betrayal of yourself. You had to learn to be a certain way in order to get what you needed for survival. And even more sadly, even when you were willing to make those trade-offs, the adults around you may not have been able to deliver on their end of the bargain. After telling you, directly or indirectly, that you had to be a certain way in order to get their love, they may not have been able to really fulfill the promise.

And so what does that conditioning teach you about life? If the adults were able to come through on their end of the bargain, then maybe you learned that love is a kind of transaction – an arrangement in which one must pay for the most basic of needs. But the payment expected of you may have been very high. You might have had to deny or betray important aspects of who you are as a soul. On the other hand, if the adults were too wounded themselves to be able to uphold their end of the deal, then you likely learned a deep sense of mistrust – that even when you are willing to surrender things that are important to you, other people can't be counted on.

Taking on the wounds of others. We pass our wounds from one generation to the next. Virtually all of us carry within the personality self several fears or resentments that we learned from mother, father, aunts, uncles, siblings, and even the culture in which we grew up. This idea is even found in the Old Testament, although with the sense of a punishing God rather than a psychological process of conditioning and wound-transmission.

> The Lord is slow to anger, and abounding in steadfast love, forgiving iniquity and transgression, but by no means clearing the guilty, visiting the iniquity of the parents upon the children to the third and the fourth generation. (Numbers 14:18.)

To a large measure the work of personal transformation is a matter of becoming aware of the wounds of others that you have taken on – starting early in life – and then the task of *giving those wounds back*. That doesn't mean payback time. Nothing is accomplished by mistreating later in life those very people who may have crippled you by expecting you to carry their burdens. Instead, the "giving back" is a *psychological* process that needs to happen inside of yourself. It is awakening to the fact that certain beliefs and practices that took root in you are not really your own. They belong to your father or mother or someone else. And as your own individuality awakens, you begin to get clear about what is really you and what belongs to others. Then there can be a metaphorical "giving back." That means your willingness to divest yourself of emotions, beliefs, resentments, or fears that you have been carrying for someone else – most often your parents.

In summary, then, we can see that the formation of the human personality is a flawed and perilous endeavor. But we live in a flawed and unhealthy society, and so it is no wonder that we emerge from childhood and adolescence and into adulthood as scarred and handicapped people – *all of us*, even those who had nice and pleasant childhoods. Some lucky few are perhaps less scarred than others, but they, too, have considerable work to do in letting go of the conditioning of early life so that the soul-self, the individuality, can emerge and flower.

Six Principles to Begin Soul Transformation Work

By seeing what might have gone wrong in the first two decades of life, we identify where much of the work of personal transformation needs to be done. Many of these experiences have to be "undone" or healed in order for soul transformation to take place in the second half of life. Let's consider some of the foundation points for that process. Six principles rest at the heart of transformative change. More superficial "self-improvement" changes can be made without engaging these six. However, changes that involve the soul-self require all of these elements.

Connection to a magnetic center. This term was coined by Gurdjieff, and it refers to an inner knowing that materiality can never explain everything. It's the intuitive grasp that realizes that there must be more to life than material conditions suggest. In fact, without this sense that "there must be something more," we're not likely to persist with genuine transformational work. Too easily we will just drop back into our comfort zones.

Whether or not we think of such a "magnetic center" as a physical place within ourselves, we can be alert for how it calls to us. In the midst of busy-ness with our stress-filled lives, it produces in us *a kind of curiosity and longing to be connected to something bigger* – to have an understanding that operates on a larger scale. It usually comes as a *feeling* rather than a thought. A magnetic center reminds us to be very careful in what we value. It deepens the conviction that physical life can never be fully understood in terms of itself – that something of a higher dimension is required.

Willingness to face pain. One of the axioms of Jung's transformational process he called individuation states this point clearly. He writes that there is no birth in consciousness without pain. Just as surely as the mother and baby experience pain in the process of physical birth, we must expect that the emergence of a new sense of self will be a painful one. But as Austrian psychiatrist Viktor Frankl, who survived the Nazi concentration camps, reminds us, we are able to undergo and survive all imaginable pain and suffering if only we see meaning and purpose in what is going on.

But what is pain anyway? Simply the other side of the coin from pleasure and happiness. Greater self-awareness will bring enhanced pleasure, joy, and well-being – but it also brings experiences of pain. The pain is bearable, though, when we understand it as part of a bigger process, when we see the purposefulness and meaning in it. As the meditation teacher Osho put it:

> If you become aware, there is suffering. If you become aware, you become aware of pain, and the pain is so much that you would like to take a tranquilizer and be asleep. This sleepiness in life works as a protection against pain. But this is the trouble – if you are asleep against pain, you are

> asleep against pleasure also.... Now you are in a dilemma. If you want no pain – immediately pleasure disappears from your life, happiness disappears. If you want happiness, you open the faucet – immediately there is pain also flowing. If you have to be aware, you have to be aware of both...If you are afraid of pain you will remain in hypnosis... Because you are afraid of pain you cannot become aware – and then you cannot learn anything. (*Tao: The Three Treasures, Vol. 4 #6 Q. 2.*)

In essence, the journey of transformation asks us to trust the flow of life, to trust awareness and where it will take us. Even though the journey is sometimes painful, there is a force that wants to take us to our longings and ideals. And if we agree to cooperate with its transformational power, then it will take us right to the places in life where its movement is blocked – right to the places where we are resisting Spirit. It's a marvelous and sometimes scary fact about personal transformation. As soon as we are willing to change, as soon as we say yes to the process, then energy moves right to the points where that energy is blocked in us: fears, resentments, guilt, judgments. Those will be places that are uncomfortable and even painful to be aware of. The test is to see whether or not you can stay present to that place that is almost unbearable. Just the willingness to stay present and aware in the face of pain allows something to begin to change.

Respect for the body and instincts. Your attitudes and feelings about your body are crucial in order to make deep personal change. There is no transformation of your being unless there is first a profound appreciation for the body. But this principle is often hard to accept. To make matters even more difficult, there are many ancient traditions that seem to disrespect the body, virtually seeing it as the enemy to soul growth. Added to that, our mainstream culture with its preoccupation with appearances, sexuality, and body image is inherently anti-body. By objectifying the physical body – making it a "thing" instead of a living instrument connected to the Spirit – the culture that surrounds us daily is deeply disrespectful toward the body and all its instinctual drives.

Soul transformation work is done on the foundation of a healthy relationship with your own body. Put into the language of the spiritual centers or chakras, we might remind ourselves that *all* seven centers are *spiritual* centers, and that our connection to so-called "higher centers" must rest upon a solid foundation with the "lower centers" that have to do with our earthliness. Unless you can truly begin to feel comfortable and at-home in your own skin, then any effort to have transcendent experiences is really just an escape and is doomed to failure in the long run.

Openness to paradox. As much as our logical minds would prefer things to be otherwise, paradox is an unavoidable mystery of soul transformation work. As soon as we try to understand the human soul, we encounter truth that seems to be self-contradictory. We find it in the teachings of the Buddha and Christ. For example, if you wish to gain your life, then you need to be willing to lose your life. If you want to know the universal, then you need to be willing to engage and be present to the smallest and most insignificant aspects of life.

The most challenging paradoxes aren't the metaphysical riddles, as perplexing as they may be. The deepest test is when you confront a paradox about yourself – when you encounter two sides of yourself that seem to contradict each other, and yet they are both true of you. Simply by letting yourself be open to the paradox – to let it work on your feeling nature instead of trying to figure it out – something can begin to change in you.

Here is one example that you may well face along your journey of personal transformation. You discover that you are very angry at a person and you are also deeply in love with that same person. How can two such opposite emotions both be true, and yet you experience the vivid reality of both. The intellect says that if you truly love someone then it should dissolve the anger; or, if you are truly angry at someone, then it should crowd out and cancel the possibility for love. But rational analysis betrays us in this example and countless other paradoxes. It is a mark of your spiritual maturity that you can hold simultaneously both sides of a contradiction about yourself.

Paradox disengages the intellect, and that's a good thing for anyone who is willing to change in a deep, transformative way. That aspect of the mind that analyzes and breaks things down to find distinctions is a wonderful tool for being practical and getting tasks done in daily life. But the rational mind is often a huge obstacle to transformation. Its cleverness usually serves just to keep the status quo. That's why the paradoxes created by higher dimensional truth are so valuable. They require the intellect to step aside and let something else come in.

Sensitivity to one's intuition. The "something else that can come in" is intuitive wisdom. Intuition is the way that you can grasp and experience the individuality self, the authentic identity that resides in your soul. It won't be through logical analysis that you initiate and sustain transformative change. Admittedly logic has a role to play, but intuition holds the key.

It's not easy to trust intuition. There is little in the everyday material world that supports making that leap. Almost everywhere you turn there seem to be good reasons to be more logical, analytical, and clever. How else can you cope with a world that is full of cunning – for example, scam artists out to steal your identity, bosses ready to squeeze more work out of you, and acquaintances all too ready to take advantage of your good intentions? Life teaches you to be on guard, and it usually seems that rational thinking is the best way to protect yourself.

However, if you are going to explore the bigger picture of what life is all about, then you are going to need to make use of the side of the mind that operates in that expanded world. That's your intuition. It finds connections that aren't evident to your intellect. Intuition is able to integrate, where the intellect is master of dissection. Intuition will be your greatest ally along the journey of personal transformation.

Willingness to meet life with the spirit of guidance. Intuition naturally brings us to the subject of guidance. There can be no deep change in ourselves unless we can allow ourselves to be touched by something bigger than ourselves. That kind of openness is the meaning of the phrase "the spirit of guidance." Of course, certain self-improvement changes may be possible by "pulling ourselves up by our own bootstraps," so to speak. We can use our smarts and our cleverness to a certain extent to make changes in ourselves, but they won't be the deep, transformational changes that the soul longs for.

That more profound work requires input from resources beyond ourselves, from beyond our own conscious understanding of things.

Transformational change depends on our willingness to be open and to receive guidance that comes from resources that are there to help – inner and outer. That can mean dream guidance or meditation guidance. It can be intuitive insights that come spontaneously or through synchronistic occurrences. Or the guidance may come from a therapist or teacher. The point is to have an openness and a willingness to receive direction from resources that come from beyond your own intellect and cleverness. *The point is to believe that such help is possible and available.*

Methods and Approaches to Support Transformative Change

Setting boundaries. The individuality self is your authentic identity. The transformation from experiencing yourself as personality to individuality starts with setting some borders between yourself and all that crowds and impinges on you. That means saying "no" to the inner *and* outer voices that tug at you. That "no" is a matter of affirming your personhood. Beneath the negation there is actually a more significant *affirmation* of something. Many of your childhood wounds probably relate to the invasiveness of others. Lots of people had expectations for you – expectations that fulfill their needs, not yours. Any tendency you may have developed in childhood to let that happen to you now needs to be transformed in adult life. That's the only way you are going to be able to have healthy, fulfilling relationships – romantic, friendship, or business.

The point is this: *there is no love and no intimacy with others unless we can first define our own boundaries.* It's a matter of the most basic practical spirituality to say "no" when we need to. Then, from that position of relative strength, we can enter into relationship with another person. As strange as it may sound to our ears, loving someone may start by stepping back from them – saying "no" and defining oneself – and *then* finding the capacity to reach out and build an authentic bridge to that person.

In daily life you can look for situations that challenge you – little tests about whether you will give in and let others define you *or* stand up for yourself. In a counseling or therapeutic setting, there are exercises designed to let you practice this skill. Those exercises can be as simple as practicing saying "no" – with vigor and intensity – to someone else, perhaps a person who is adamantly saying "no" right back to you. Even an exercise as simple as this might be scary for you because most of us have so little practice in daily life with standing up for ourselves in a balanced, healthy way.

Recognizing longings and ideals. Your capacity to truly change something about your life depends on having a clear sense of ideal. There needs to be a longing in the heart for a new way of being. Remember from Chapter 1 the description of four phases in the transformative journey – a model based on a drawing by Rudolf Steiner. The first phase is "Catching the Vision." That's the step of recognizing what your heart longs for at this point in your life.

So, how do you connect to your longings and ideals? First you have to be able to drop any obligation to what *other people* are longing to have you do. That's a matter of saying "no," as mentioned above. Then there can be room to feel for yourself. Maybe that means letting memories come back to you about times in your life when your heart was able to sing. What were you doing then, what kind of a person were you being in those situations from the past? The memories may give you clues about what you heart is longing for in the months and years ahead.

The recognition of longings and ideals can also be powerfully revealed through dreams. That's *not* to say that everything you dream about doing is a reflection of your deepest ideals. Admittedly, some of your dreams are sure to reflect superficial desires and old habit patterns. But if you will watch your dreams closely over a period of weeks and months, you are sure to find that occasionally a dream emerges that has a qualitatively different flavor. Such a dream feels like it comes from your depths. There will be something about who you are in that dream that feels like it is coming from an authentic place inside you that rarely gets noticed. The dream may or may not depict you doing something; the dream may or may not be direct guidance about what you could be doing in your life to find greater fulfillment and joy. What's more important, though, is not so much the "doing" as it is the "being." What are the feelings that surface from a dream like that? What is your sense of yourself, your sense of who you are? Those kinds of dreams can be powerful clues for recognizing the longings that can inspire and direct your personal transformation.

Bringing needed props and support into place. Every one of us needs support in order to change. It's one thing to be willing to change. It's another story to be able to make that change happen. Success often depends on putting in place the support that you need.

But even the word "support" may leave you with mixed feelings. On the one hand it sounds great, but you may find yourself saying, "I don't want to end up feeling dependent on someone else, or feeling like I owe someone because of how they have supported me." But the kind of support that is crucial for personal transformation is not dependency (or co-dependency). In fact, the necessary support may not even come from another person. But when it does, the support can be purposeful and non-entangling – if both parties are clear about intentions.

Consider why we even need support in the first place. It is very difficult to stay with one's "edge," one's growing edge for transformation. An edge is a tender, vulnerable, uncomfortable place. Your tendency will be to avoid going to such a place inside yourself; or, finding yourself at an edge you're likely to try to escape from it as soon as you can. Support can help you stick with it, to hang-in-there and be present to the emotions and attitudes that surface as you courageously try to face an old wound. The support may be a friend or therapist or group. The support may be a teaching or philosophy. The support can just as easily be a place to which you can retreat – your garden or study or forest pathway.

An analogy from hatha yoga demonstrates how support works. The very idea of being at an "edge" comes from the practice of yoga. It's the point in an asana (or posture) at which you are feeling stretched, but not yet in pain that causes spasm or injury. As you bring your body's movement right to that edge and hold it with awareness, conscious breathing, and attention, then something might be able to shift and move for you. Perhaps that conscious presence toward an edge allows a gentle change to take place, and you stretch just a little bit farther. But for that to happen, it's sometimes useful to have a so-called "prop," such as a block. The prop supports you so that you can stay right at that edge. It even allows you to relax into that edge. It's not doing the work for you; it's simply making it possible for you to more effectively do the work of attention and presence.

Seeing what makes you lose your power – how you leak energy. To change you need energy. In fact, lack of energy virtually ensures the status quo. And so, one powerful method to support the work of personal transformation is to start recognizing how you lose energy – how you "leak energy" in a variety of ways. More often than not, the biggest step is simply *seeing more consciously* what you are doing. Making the necessary changes afterwards may be a small step. The problem comes from how *unconscious* we are of the give-aways we are making all the time. Of course, you may know about these tendencies, but it's usually after the fact. In the moment that the energy is leaking out, you are probably entranced by the hypnotic-like power of those patterns.

There are two principal categories at play here. You leak *energy to other people* when you let their agendas and their needs blind you from your own. That's not to say that you have to become hard-hearted and selfish in order to stop leaking energy. But when the demands of others drown out any sensitivity to your own needs, then you can be sure that you are losing your power and staying stuck in your ruts.

A second category is completely internal. There are *voices in your own mind that undercut you.* Sometimes the self-betrayal is direct, such as a voice that tries to make you feel guilty and leaves you weakened and in despair. But other times this self-sabotage is subtle. For example, you might be losing energy by continually following "The Pusher" voice inside you, the voice that says that you always have to be accomplishing more. You might even feel a little bit proud of that voice, not understanding how insidious it really is. Indirectly that voice is saying that you aren't good enough just as you are, and that you have to prove yourself with super-human accomplishments. What ends up happening is an extraordinary amount of energy invested in busy-work and achievements that have little to do with really helping anyone – including yourself.

Making space for yourself. When we think about the word "space" it usually brings to mind physical space, room to spread out or roam. In other words, it's the opposite of feeling claustrophobic. But even more important is *psychological* space – that is, room internally to experience one's own feelings and thoughts. There is a psychological claustrophobia that's even worse than the physical version. When old "tapes" and inner voices are crowding in on you, how can you expect to actually feel your own being?

Some of the most important methods of transformational work involve creating the inner space that you need to find a new sense of who you are. It's like making a clearing in the woods – letting the sunlight in and making room to build a safe, new home for yourself. When the forest is thick and impenetrable, what hope is there for ever feeling safe and at peace? A clear space is needed, and that takes some work.

Obviously, this fifth method is reminiscent of the first – setting boundaries. Both involve defining oneself and distinguishing between what is one's own stuff and what belongs to others. The first one, however, is somewhat more masculine in tone. It asks us to say "no" and create some borders. It gives you the feeling of taking back your power. In contrast, to make space for yourself has a somewhat more feminine tone. Now the purpose for the borders becomes more evident. Something that is womb-like comes into being. The new psychological space is a creative arena. It's a place in which creation is invited to weave its mysterious magic. Just like boundary-setting, it reconnects you to your own power, but now it's also a power bigger than yourself that has a chance to work in and through you.

So exactly how do you go about making space for yourself? There are several therapeutic exercises that can be done in a group setting or with a therapist or counselor. But there are also things that you can do on your own. All of these methods involve enhancing your awareness of the influences that crowd in on you that take up your psychological space with their demands, expectations, or guilt-inducing voices. Maybe it can be useful to draw a symbolic picture of the forces in your life that squeeze you and make you feel trapped. Dreamwork can help identify many of the subtle influences that entrap you and limit your freedom. Or, if you're working in a group setting with a therapist, this question might be explored through role playing in which various members of the group are asked to stand in for certain inner and outer voices in your life that take up your space.

However, the enhancement of your awareness about space-reducers isn't the whole story. You still need to find ways to diminish the effects of those influences. First, it's a matter of saying "no" in whatever way is required. But it's also a matter of finding *proactive* ways to actually *take* the space you need. For example, it's not enough just to become more aware of and say "no" to an inner voice (perhaps created early in your childhood) that says, "You're not good enough, you're not worthy." The next step is to proactively support that nascent new space by adopting attitudes *and* ways of acting that reflect the transformative change you long for. To make space for yourself, you may need to find a new voice that says, "I have my own, unique talents, and I'm worthy to explore where they will take me." That inner posture supports the space you are making for yourself. So, too, will actions that express the new attitude. Maybe that means setting aside a place in your home to do your artistic work. Maybe it means sitting down every Sunday evening with your appointment book, looking at the week ahead, and carving out the time you want to invest in exploring your talents. Whatever form it may take, the important thing is to act in a way that reinforces and supports the new space that you are courageously claiming.

Finding constructive use of anger. Personal transformation requires that you connect with your fire. Without the energy of passion, you are likely to settle back into your comfort zone. But if you are like most of us, you're a little scared of anger – your own and the anger of others. That might be because of childhood experiences of being the target of anger – direct anger or passive-aggressive anger. Or maybe you've had some experiences with your own anger as an adult, and you're convinced that it can be only destructive.

In spite of reasonable misgivings, you need to learn to go back and reconnect to your fiery power. You may need to learn some strong ways to stand up for yourself – even occasionally tell people in no uncertain terms where you stand or how you expect to be treated. But more important than any spewing of your anger is the need to find safe containers where it can be experienced and lived out purposefully and cleanly.

This is not a recommendation to start being rude. The world already has enough in-your-face, rude people. But as we saw earlier, transformative change requires the capacity to say "no" and to define your boundaries. Most often it probably suffices just to state a firm "no," letting it be known who you are and how you need to be treated. But sometimes you may need to show a little fire.

Anger is an emotion directly related to saying "no" to what's going on. You don't need to run around blowing your stack daily, but you do need to be sufficiently connected to your personal power so that you can get angry in the right way when the occasion calls for it. As one piece of wisdom from the spiritual philosophy of Edgar Cayce puts it: "Be angry but sin not. For he that never is angry is worth little." But then he adds the importance of having a *container* for that anger. "But he that is angry and controlleth it not is worthless." (1156-1) Note here that "control" does not mean "suppression" but instead "proper direction." It's a crucial distinction.

Maybe sometimes we're just trying too hard to be nice. In fact, "niceness" can be a mask for a lot of unresolved feelings, such as low self-esteem and fear. Admittedly niceness is sometimes an authentic expression of untainted love that arises out of inner strength. (And for a few very healthy people, "niceness" may be just that virtually all of the time.) But a majority of us suffer from some degree of *compulsive niceness*, and often it's the way we put off dealing with life head-on. We're nice because we don't want to hurt someone's feelings, when in fact they need something else far more than having feelings protected: they need genuine human encounter that is honest and purposeful. But that takes a lot of energy, and it's risky. It's usually the safer bet just to be nice – to avoid getting angry and standing up for yourself – and let the situation pass. That's settling for the comfort zone.

And so, what kind of world will we have if individuals are able *consciously* to get angry, to say "no," and to even occasionally to tell people to "Go to hell"? In many ways "conscious anger" would make for a healthy, saner world – perhaps even one with *less* antagonism and negativity, simply because we would have less bottled up and repressed energy leaking out in insidious ways.

Conclusions

The challenges of the second half of life are daunting. It's so easy just to go with the drift of events. Why bother to try changing things when it takes so much effort and the results aren't guaranteed? Why go back and deal with difficulties and traumas from the distant past – even to open up old wounds?

Those tough questions have a direct answer: the longings of your heart won't be fulfilled otherwise. Unless you are willing to change, unless you are courageous enough to take a journey of personal transformation, then it's highly unlikely that you'll be able to attain what your soul longs for. The work is worth it.

To a certain extent the wounds must be opened. They are still festering beneath the surface. You are infected with resentments, guilt, and sadness; and even if your personality self has created clever masks to hide it from others (and from yourself), your daily living is still deeply affected by these patterns from the past. Once your wounds are open there is the possibility of healing. The willingness to face yourself and share yourself as you really are is the way of transformation. That which we hide has power over us; that which we are willing to look at and expose (in the context of loving support) then loses any power to control us.

The wounds can be opened in a safe way, however. Most important is a clear ideal and intention for this inner work. Equally important is a strong sense that there are powerful forces within you and outside you that are ready to help this transformation process. Then it's a matter of forcing safe "containers" in which to do this work – individuals and groups that will truly support you.

Parts II and III of this book will take you deeper into this exploration of the transformation process. In Part II you'll learn about the transformation of time and the practice of meditation as two of the most powerful allies you can have along this journey. Then in Part III, you get an in-depth look at perhaps your most important resource for change: a healthy free will.

Part II:

MAPS AND METHODS FOR SOUL TRANSFORMATION

Chapter 3

The Transformation of Time

"Heaven is nowhere in space, but it is in time."
Sir Arthur Stanley Eddington (1882-1944)
British physicist and astronomer

Time travel is one of the favorite plot devices of science fiction novelists and moviemakers. They know that we are drawn to the idea of getting beyond the limits of time. Commonsense logic tells us that the past is unchangeable and the future unknowable. But something else stirs in us to suggest otherwise. Maybe – just maybe – time isn't as linear and rigid as we normally think.

We get hints of the deeper mystery of time in subtle ways. A precognitive dream. A déjà vu experience. If we pay close attention to our inner and outer lives, there seem to be clues hinting that time is more than we've thought.

But what are our chances of truly understanding how time works? Modern physics presents a dizzying analysis of time, one that leaves room for relativistic time frames that move at different paces and, more mystifying, the possibility that time can in essence move backward. Can we really figure all this out, or would it require us to have the mind of God? Perhaps it is ultimately beyond our reach. Huston Smith, author of *The Religions of Man*, offered an apt analogy. The gap between human consciousness and divine consciousness is probably like the gap between the canine consciousness of our pet dog and the consciousness of a human. There are simply some human things that dogs are never going to be able to understand.

But before we give up trying, let's consider how time is surely at the heart of the question of how we change. We confront it in so many ways as soon as we feel even the smallest willingness to change. How long will change take? When am I really ready to begin the transformation process? How will I deal with the inevitable tendency to procrastinate in getting around to really doing what I need to do in order to change?

However, those questions are just a superficial way in which time and change are irrevocably linked. In this chapter we will explore a deeper and more profound principle – one that may even strike you as disturbing because of the way it turns upside-down the way you normally see life. The principle states that genuine transformation is possible only if you awaken to a deeper understanding of the nature of time – even that time is not linear (a timeline) the way your conscious personality is sure to see it. This exploration becomes a mysterious and mind-boggling adventure into reconsidering how past, present, and future are linked. It examines how certain aspects of modern day physics (particularly quantum mechanics) sounds a lot like classical mysticism and its teaching that "all time is one time."

Autobiographical Perspectives on Time and Transformation

I started off to be a physicist. I received a scholarship to a prestigious science and engineering school, Rice University, planning to become a physicist. At eighteen I was full of enthusiasm to be a scientist. But in my own personal journey, I discovered transpersonal psychology, parapsychology, and Eastern mysticism at about the same time I was preparing to start my university education. And I wasn't exactly sure what to do with what I was learning from my self-directed studies in these fields, especially parapsychology (the scientific study of psychic ability). Its findings often seemed to be so contrary to what I knew I would be learning in my university physics classes.

In spite of those doubts and concerns, life often has a certain momentum of its own, and I sincerely set out on a college education to become a mainstream scientist. After a couple of years, I changed course, settling on psychology as a compromise between science and spirituality. From my personal studies I had found convincing evidence that there was a much bigger picture of reality than I was likely to be taught in university physics classes.

One resource in particular during this part of my life story was especially significant – the study of the work of Christian spiritual philosopher and clairvoyant, Edgar Cayce, who worked in the first half of the twentieth century. He is not usually thought of as a contributor to in-depth discussions about the nature of time and space. But as a seer and clairvoyant – we might even call him a mystic - he is a fascinating case study, demonstrating much of what cutting-edge physics might say is theoretically possible for human consciousness.

I particularly liked the word *seer* to describe who Cayce was. Harmon Bro is the one scholar who identified Cayce this way, and his biography of Cayce is entitled *A Seer Out of Season*. But if we think of the word *seer* as one who can perceive or see with the "inner eye," we can imagine that much of Cayce's clairvoyant work was seeing into the multi-dimensionality of time. I remember when I first encountered his teachings on the nature of time. I had trouble knowing what to do with repeated statements such as "All time is one time - see? That is as a fact..." (294-45). I vigorously resisted the notion. It seemed to me that if we throw out the familiar concept of time, then a lot of other concepts have to be dismissed also –ideas like soul development and accountability. They appear to depend on a past that is over and done with, and a future that is yet to be created.

But over the years I have slowly come around to accept the idea that a radically new idea of time is required if we hope to understand how the universe is structured and how we meet the practical challenges of spirituality and personal transformation. In spite of the way that it seems to fly in the face of commonsense, the evidence simply seems too strong to dispute – especially some of the recent discoveries from sub-atomic physics research – the observation of sub-atomic processes that seem to clearly defy our everyday notion of a one-dimensional timeline. Time appears to be far more complex than some timeline on which the great and trivial events of history are irrevocably ordered.

The teachings of spiritual philosophers G.I. Gurdjieff and P.D. Ouspensky became the next important resource for my own evolving sense of what time is all about. It was their rediscovery and renewal of certain ancient philosophical teachings about time that were pivotal for me. It helped me see that the very nature of time is central to understanding how authentic personal transformation is possible.

Clues from Ancient Philosophy about Time and Transformation

Ouspensky points out that there are intriguing references to the nature of time in certain Hermetic traditions, a little-understood philosophy that is traced back to the mysterious character, Hermes. The Hermetic wisdom tradition is not per se Christian or really associated with any religious tradition. But in the early first, second, and third centuries A.D. it took on a certain Neoplatonic flavor, and in the Renaissance it resurfaced with much of alchemy. Several twentieth century philosophers, many of them deeply influenced by Gurdjieff and Ouspensky, have brought a new appreciation for Hermetic teachings to our own times.

For example, one especially noteworthy book is Jacob Needleman's *Time and the Soul.* Needleman proposes that these ancient teachings are trying to awaken us to the fact that we misunderstand time. We are filled with illusions about who we are, including our basic identity and the extent to which we have any power or freedom. Even more significantly he insists that we cannot grasp the meaning of these ancient teachings about time unless we realize they are more fundamentally telling us something about *ourselves.* Needleman writes that their teachings about the mirage of time are actually a reflection of what goes on inside of ourselves – in a sense, a fundamental misunderstanding about ourselves.

> What is said about time in the wisdom traditions of the world cannot be separated from the teachings about the Self. If we make the mistake of separating these two, if we limit our interests to the philosophical question of time without also attending to the question of truth about ourselves, we'll never be able to receive the help offered by these great teachings and philosophies. (pages 112-113)

Any willingness on our part to change – any sense that personal transformation is something worthy of our commitment – means a willingness to see through the illusions and distortions we have about ourselves. The ancient Hermetic teachings (which we will explore in more detail soon) and Needleman's contemporary rendition of some of them, point to the fact that *we are unlikely to experience genuine transformation unless we are willing to rethink what time itself is all about*.

A good starting place for that rethinking is to consider that time isn't really one-dimensional – it isn't merely a line along which we can move in only one direction. But what *is* a "dimension" anyway? It's a way of measurement. If you know how many measurements it takes to adequately describe something's character, then you have found its dimensionality. As a somewhat fanciful example, if you're a bridge player you know that a bid is two-dimensional because it requires both a number and a suit – for example, 2-clubs or 4-diamonds. In other words, playing the card game of bridge, a bid is two-dimensional.

Many metaphysical and spiritual philosophies agree that human experience is fundamentally three-dimensional, and so we tend to structure our view of reality in terms of three measurements. And so we see physical space in terms of height, width, and depth. Our everyday consciousness sees time as past, present, and future. We tend to see the Godhead in terms of a Trinity, and the list just goes on and on – ways we just naturally gravitate to structures that are three measurements.

Familiar waking consciousness is sometimes referred to as "local awareness," as opposed to the "non-local awareness" of a clairvoyant or mystic. It is called "local" because we have the sense that anything that can be known must be within the range of our physical senses – for example, all we can know of time is the present moment. "Local awareness" therefore creates what Maurice Nicoll (author of *Living Time*) calls momentary psychology, a kind of psychology of this moment. In our everyday consciousness we can understand only this moment as having reality. Events that "have been" are absolutely not "real" anymore. The past is just a memory or an entry in the history books. The past is essentially dead, at least according to "momentary psychology." What's more, things that haven't manifested yet also don't really have reality. The future is ephemeral and has no substance or genuine meaning. Hence, we have a momentary psychology in our day-to-day affairs, no matter how much we may have a respect for the past or how much we are intrigued by what the future could bring. Our physical senses tell us that only this moment is real.

But mystics for thousands of years (and consciousness researchers from modern times) assert that there is another consciousness available to us constantly: a "non-local awareness" that goes beyond those limits. We can transcend one-dimensional, momentary psychology. As Nicoll writes in *Living Time*,

> We witness events, people and things disappearing into total extinction, into absolute nothingness as a result of passing time. It's kind of in an annihilated time ... For all this seeming loss of everything – the fear of losing, the apparent uselessness of so much that we undertake and cannot finish, the confused sense of missed opportunities, the feeling of hurrying in life, and the thought of the impossibility of going back and altering anything – all this combines to create one distinct picture of existence, a way of understanding it, and a certain feeling of oneself, a certain feeling of "I." (p. 104)

The transformation of our sense of time can, in turn, give us a transformed sense of ourselves. In fact, it may well be that unless we can learn how to step out of "momentary psychology" - out of "the sense of passing time"- then the full potential of transformation can never be realized. *In order to change deeply we must gain a new feeling for time and hence a new feeling of oneself.*

But what is this different "feeling of oneself?" It's not just a different intellectual understanding of who you are, but instead a *different experience* of your own identify. Consider again Nicoll's litany of the feelings of oneself created by passing time. See if this characterizes your life, because if it does, you are embedded in what we described in Chapter 2 as the personality, as opposed to individuality. Passing time or momentary psychology is the hallmark of the personality. Does this sound like your life?

- The fear of losing.
- The apparent uselessness of so much that we undertake and can't finish.
- The confused sense of having missed out on opportunities.
- The feeling of hurrying through life.

- The thought of the impossibility of going back and altering anything.

All these characteristics of modern life are often what painfully push us to the point of even being willing to change. They combine to create a certain feeling about self, and that feeling can become to be so stifling and inauthentic that something deep in us calls out and demands some kind of transformation.

Returning then to the question of dimensions, what happens if we try to understand the so-called three-dimensional world we experience in daily life? And exactly what are those three dimensions, anyway – what are those three essential measurements? Edgar Cayce's philosophy has a novel angle on the issue, saying that the three dimensions of human experience are time, space, and patience – an idea that sounds curious, especially that third measurement, patience. How could "patience" be a dimension? It is seemingly a moralistic concept – something you were told by authority figures: "You've got to be patient; you've got to wait." By what stretch of the imagination is "patience" a fundamental measuring rod of our human experiences – something as essential as time and space?

The answer comes from realizing that patience isn't really about waiting. Instead, it's about being present – truly present, with one's attention *and* intention. "In patience do we possess our souls" simply because patience is related to our connection to ideals, values, and intentions. And when we can be fully present and attentive to our own ideals, values, and intentions, then a whole different feeling of ourselves emerges. Of course, the word patience is really just a placeholder for an entire arena of human experience – namely, *our responses to what is going on around us in time and space*. And more often than not, that response is frustration, resistance, and fear – hardly qualities that will lead to a connection to the soul or facilitate any kind of personal transformation. Consider this analogy:

> Imagine that at lunchtime I invite you to go with me down to the bank, the one we both do business with. We both have some transactions that need to be done there, and so we go there together over the lunch hour. Upon arrival we find that two tellers have their windows open, and for each teller

there is a line of five people. The lines are moving very, very slowly. People have brought all kinds of complex transactions, and it's going to take us a long time to ever get up there so we can do our business.

Now, on the one hand, you and I are having similar experiences as a soul. The time component is identical – say, 12:15 p.m. on Friday, November 11, 2005 A.D. What's more the spatial dimension is virtually identical – say, in the lobby of the Bank of America, at Pacific Avenue and 31st Street. At least in terms of those two dimensions we're having pretty much the same experience.

And yet let's suppose I'm standing in line and I can see no purposefulness to what's going on here. I'm frustrated, I'm angry, I'm feeling offended. On the other hand, imagine that you're having the same experience in time and space, but you've decided there must be some purposefulness for why you're standing there. You let yourself drop into being present to your values and ideals. You're present with your attention, aware that a meaningful opportunity could be found in the current situation. Maybe the person in line in front of you is somebody with whom you are meant to have a conversation. Something beautiful could emerge out of that. And you've decided just to be with the experience and make something out of it that might surprise you.

In essence, we are having very different experiences as a soul, even though that annoying little video camera up on the ceiling watching to make sure that we're not bank robbers would record something that looks about the same. But something very different is going on in the two of us because of the dimension of "patience."

Intentionality, Eternity, and the Transformation of Time

So how do these three dimensions of time, space, and patience inter-relate? How is authentic change – deep personal transformation – possible in the three-dimensional experience of material life? The way that we experience time itself is surely one of the keys. And so, too, is the power of ideals and intention – or best we say "intentionality."

Intentionality is something deeper than intention. You can claim to have the intention to be a nicer person or get up earlier in the morning – but that's like a New Year's resolution, and we know what usually happens to them. However, intentionality is something deeper. It engages the unconscious as well as the conscious self. Intentionality is the ideal that lives within the soul, and it's something much more significant than the little intentions and plans we make. More often than not our intentions are just mimicking back our conditioning from parents and teachers and the society around us. But an authentic ideal, or what philosophers call intentionality, is something that arises from within the soul – something that can either be ignored or embraced.

We explored this theme in Chapter 1 in the study of the four-fold journey of transformation. That first stage along the journey is "Catching the Vision" – which is to say, responding to the intentionality within the soul, listening to its calling, seeing what is possible for the next phase of life.

So, how then, is the nature of time related to our capacity to "catch the vision," to embrace the intentionality that already lives inside us, to willingly make the transformative changes necessary to move ahead in our lives? And what does time have to do with all this? Simply this: *Opening to the oneness of all time allows us to begin to feel ourselves in a new way. And as we let ourselves feel differently, then we begin to remember the sense of life purpose and intentionality that has been there all along. Then transformative change in ourselves becomes immediately accessible.*

That deep sense of purpose, vision, and calling is most often invisible for us. We are so powerfully influenced by our wounds – such as those described in Chapter 2 – that we move around through life in a trance. To compensate for our wounds, we have cluttered our lives with all kinds of projects and intentions. We have been hypnotized by momentary psychology, which believes that time is just a line along which we can move in only one direction. A radically new way of experiencing time can change all that. But it's unnerving and sounds like the stuff of science fiction. Reassuringly, though, it *also* sounds like what the mystics and sages have been telling us for thousands of years.

Let's start examining this radically different understanding of time by considering the word "eternity." What does it mean to us? For most of us it has connotations of being extremely far off in time. The notion of a timeline is embedded in our schooling and conditioning, and so most of us try to conceptualize eternity as a place or a region on that timeline – far off on the arrow of time – at the opposite extreme from the primordial past. But Ouspensky, for one, teaches that "eternity" isn't a place along that one-dimensional timeline. He suggests that's a false way of understanding eternity. Instead, it's fully present in this moment – in *every* moment – if we're open to experience it. Eternity is a second dimension that cuts perpendicularly through *every* moment of passing time. If we can be fully present – if we can be "patient" and be open to ourselves as souls – then at *any* moment we can have the experience of eternity, the feeling that time is not at all the rigid master of our lives. Returning for another installment of the banking analogy:

> I'm standing there in the Bank of America lobby, in the left-hand teller line fuming because of how offended I feel. "Didn't they know I was coming?" I think to myself. "If there was any justice in the world, they would have opened a third teller line that said 'For Mark Thurston Only.'" But you are standing in the right teller line, just being present to what's happening, just being able to see this moment as a wonderful moment, as a purposeful moment, alert for something that could happen because of the way this moment is structured. You're in eternity. I'm stuck in Hell.

Ouspensky continues and offers a fascinating model of time as having three-dimensions of its own. This is not easy for the intellectual mind to grasp, so just play with these ideas for yourself and see how they stimulate your intuition and feelings. He asks us to consider that time has three dimensions, just as space has its three dimensions of height, width, and depth. So what are time's three dimensions?

The first dimension of time is the one that's already familiar to us – the timeline of passing time as we usually think of it. What's more, that timeline, when added to the three dimensions of space creates a four dimensional world, which he calls "higher space." Imagine, for example, having a psychic experience or a dream in which you experience vividly a place that existed five years ago but is no longer around. That "space" you were in seemed so real. But when you came out of the psychic experience or woke up from the dream, it all seemed impossible because that place doesn't exist anymore. But perhaps this was simply a fourth dimensional experience, and maybe your capacity to experience isn't locked rigidly into what your physical senses can perceive right now.

Ouspensky goes on to say that there's a second dimension to time. As an analogy, time now becomes like a surface, not just a line. And once we have a surface, that second dimension allows us to draw not just a straight line but a circle. Hence we have the possibility of cycles of time or recurrent patterns of time – something found in many indigenous cultures. A second dimension of time also begins to answer the question of how we can experience things happening to us that have *already* occurred – recurrence or déjà vu. "Wait a minute. I've been through this before!"

Many have offered explanations for déjà vu, generally very unsatisfactory explanations. Maybe the mind can dream precognitively, and you didn't remember the dream; then, when the event happens, it triggers a vague sense that you'd been through this before. Part of what makes that such an unsatisfactory answer is that it begs the question of how the mind could even dream precognitively in the first place. What is the nature of time that even makes precognition a possibility?

Or, neuroscience has suggested that maybe déjà vu is just some flaw in how the brain is wired. Normally, a new experience will seem novel because when we "check our memory banks" there is no indication this has ever happened before. But things go inexplicably haywire sometimes and the brain gets confused. The sensory impressions of some experiences were received and got stored in memory before you could check to see if it was already there. And when your conscious mind checked its memory banks, it mistakenly finds evidence to suggest "this has all happened to me before." An intriguing explanation, but for most of us who have had multiple occasions of déjà vu, it just doesn't seem like the right answer. Far more promising is Ouspensky's idea that a second dimension of time itself is involved.

But then, Ouspensky tries to stretch us a little more, saying that maybe there is even a *third* dimension to time. Even he now admits that the model is getting very difficult to grasp. Time doesn't just turn on itself in circles and cycles. There can be movement and change and growth. A third dimension of time makes possible a spiral.

Another way of trying to understand this third dimension of time would be to say that with the spiral we are freed from the never-ending repetition that happens with a two-dimensional circle. A third dimension of time makes growth and spiritual evolution possible. Recurrent patterns don't have to be continually lived with the same consciousness - repeated in what the East has for centuries called karma or what modern Western psychology calls conditioning. A realm of possibilities and alternative futures is made possible.

Of course, all of this really stretches our imagination, just as it would be for a two-dimensional "man" living in the flatland of the surface of a paper, who is challenged to understand the higher dimensional reality of solid objects that have height, width, and depth.

Evidence for Higher Dimensions of Time

Parapsychology – the scientific study of psychic ability, including the time-bending experience of precognition or prophecy – has produced some fascinating evidence that time is not linear. Under certain laboratory conditions there have been remarkable demonstrations of the capacity of some people to predict future "random events" with an accuracy that cannot be explained with any one-dimensional model of time.

But often what is even more convincing to us is a personal experience or a remarkable anecdote. The most dramatic instance of recurrence – as Ouspensky called it – that I have ever encountered was the by-product of my participation in a lengthy radio interview in Detroit about ESP some 25 years ago. When the program ended, the talk show host asked me if I could stick around for a few minutes and listen to one of her own experiences, which I readily agreed to do, not suspecting what an amazing example of non-linear time it would be.

As she told the story: "When I was fourteen years old, I had a recurrent dream, and it happened over the course of about nine months, at least a half dozen times. And in this recurrent dream, I'm in a car with a sixteen-year-old guy who, in waking life, really was my boyfriend. In the dream we had gone out to a park that's there in our city. It was at dusk, and we were sitting in this park in the car kissing.

"In the dream – as it always happened the same way every time – there is a commotion, and I look up to see a Chinese or Korean girl climbing up on the hood of the car. She's pressing her face into the windshield. And my boyfriend gets so mad in the dream that he jumps out of the car and starts screaming at her. She climbs off the car, and she's backing up and backing up to get away from him. She forgets that there's a retaining wall and a lake right there and she falls back into the lake. And then my boyfriend is so scared by what he's done that he runs back to the car, jumps in, starts up the engine and we speed out of the park. Soon thereafter we're chased by a policeman because we're going so fast and we get a speeding ticket." End of the dream.

Sitting there in the radio studio, telling me this recurrent dream from eleven years ago, she said that it must have happened at least half a dozen times and finally she told her mother about it. Of course, we can guess how a mother might interpret a dream like this, especially because she probably wasn't too fond of the idea of her daughter having a boyfriend at only fourteen. The mother's response was, "Get that boy out of your life! Nothing good could happen with this relationship." But, of course, a fourteen year old is not about to take advice like that. But after a while, as is typical for a teenage romance, the sixteen year old boy and the fourteen year old girl grew apart.

She went on to finish high school, went off to college, got her degree in communications, moved away, and got a job in radio. At twenty-five, not many months before I was on her radio show, she went back to visit her parents for a long weekend, and she saw one of her high school girl friends in the grocery store. They got to talking about people and friends that they had known in high school, and the subject came up about the person who had been her boyfriend when she was fourteen. The friend announced, "Oh, he still lives around here. I see him from time to time. You two ought to get together again."

"Oh, I don't know," the radio show hostess said, expressing some misgivings about seeing this young man again after eleven years. But, sure enough, the next day she got a call from him, apparently because the friend had in fact seen him and said, "Call her. She's back in town."

He invited her to go out to dinner, and to make a long story short, after dinner they ended up in his car at the city park at dusk sitting in the car. As she told me the story, "One thing led to the next, and before long we were kissing." Suddenly she began to feel the car rocking a little bit, and she looked up and she saw a young teenager – she guessed to be twelve or thirteen – starting to climb up on the car. But this young person was a Down Syndrome child, and she could see across the park about two hundred yards away that the parents were anxiously calling out, "Get off the car" as they hurried to catch up to her.

It was at that moment that she remembered the long-ago-forgotten recurrent dream. She had long since put it out of her mind. Her old boyfriend started to get out of the car, obviously very upset that this commotion was breaking into something more interesting to him. But she grabbed his arm and said, "You are not getting out of this car!"

"What are you talking about?"

She replied, "Roll the window down and talk the girl off the car. You are *not* getting out of the car." So he rolled the window down, and coaxed the Down Syndrome child off the car.

Then the young woman said, "Let's get out of here. I'll explain all this to you in a little while," and off they went. And before she could explain all this to him, they were caught by a traffic cop in a speed trap, pulled over and given a ticket.

I was amazed at this story. It was told to me with such sincerity, I had every reason to believe its veracity. And she seemed shaken, just in recounting the events. She wanted me to explain to her how this could be – how could time be so altered? How could she have dreamed something precognitive – in such detail – eleven years in advance? I didn't have any simple answer for her; there *is* no simple answer, especially none that the logical mind can accept because it operates on the assumptions of one-dimensional, linear time. This woman had had a profoundly disturbing experience of the complexity of time. If nothing else the experience was powerfully showing her that there is more to reality than material consciousness would suggest.

But there is one striking fact in her mind-boggling experience. At age twenty-five, things didn't really turn out the way that she had dreamed them recurrently eleven years before. Certainly there was a startling number of similarities; however, the young girl who looked oriental (or who was actually Down Syndrome) didn't end up in the lake. Once the recurrent dream was recalled, sensitive actions led to a different outcome. In other words, free will is still at play (a topic that will become a central focus for the last four chapters of this book). At best, the precognition could indicate only a possibility for how things would unfold – *one of several possible outcomes.*

Telling me this dream was unnerving for the young woman. I could see that when she brought back to mind all that had happened, the events continued to shake her. The story upset her normal assumptions about how life works. *The experience was giving her a radically different feeling about time, and even more important, it was offering her an altered feeling of herself* – someone who is part of a bigger, purposeful plan for life, yet someone who still has considerable free will in shaping how that plan actually plays out.

What a powerful insight this can be to any of us. Time is somehow "living" and multi-dimensional. We are not stuck in passing time that goes in only one direction. It's the experience that one's entire life is, in a sense, all going on "now."

One of my own dreams has shed some light on this phenomenon, at least for me. In this dream I was shown what it's like to die. Of course, that may sound rather audacious, and the picture given in my dream is hardly the only way this ancient riddle could be addressed. My experience is somewhat reminiscent of a repeated finding in the investigation of near-death experiences: a life review in which all the details of one's life are presented in detail and simultaneously.

In my dream I was moving on foot to a place back in the forest. I realized that this place in the woods was going to be the site for some kind of a very special gathering. And I was moving with great purposefulness along a trail through the forest. I could feel that just ahead there would be a clearing, and something very momentous was going to take place. And then I began to see that there were other people going to the same place. They were walking along their own little foot trails through this same forest, and I began to catch glimpses of some of them through the trees. We were converging, all of us like spokes of a wheel, moving toward the center point.

Initially, I couldn't see the identities of those other people; but as we drew nearer and nearer to the clearing in the woods and they were closer and closer to me, I could start to recognize them. *Each one was me*. Each one was Mark at a different age in my life. Fifteen-year-old Mark was there, thirty-five-year old Mark was there; even, three-year-old Mark. All these Marks were showing up at this clearing. And once we were all assembled, I intuitively realized with full clarity that this was about to be the moment of death. We had come back together for this reunion, for this "re-membering," as a way to pass into another phase of life. Death was to be not just a "re-membering" and "re-collection" but also a "remembering" and a "recollection." All the pieces of who I have been were coming back together. I was becoming aware of the wholeness of who I am.

What's more, in this remarkable dream, I also knew that the simultaneous existence of all these "Marks" was not just at the moment of death as we came together and could see each other. Just as surely, the simultaneous selves have always existed, even though momentary psychology or passing time has allowed me to be conscious of just one at a given moment.

Living Time

Psychiatrist and personal transformation expert Maurice Nicoll is an extraordinary figure of the twentieth century. For many years he was a colleague and protégé of C. G. Jung. Then he met Ouspensky and Gurdjieff and was so profoundly influenced by their work that he eventually became one of the most eloquent teachers and writers of their system of transformation. His book *Living Time* is now out-of-print, but it still constitutes one of the finest explanations of how the transformation of our understanding of time can lead to profound changes in ourselves.

Nicoll asks us to consider the question of how we conceive of ourselves. We see bodies having three spatial dimensions and existing in the moment of time we call the present. But he reminds us that this is just the appearance of things. If we can stretch our understanding and begin to conceive of ourselves four-dimensionally, then we pass beyond just the appearance of things and penetrate into a deeper realm. Now the ordinary feelings of "I" change, and a kind of personal transformation becomes a possibility. But for all of this to happen, we must come to understand the past and the future might actually be experienced as "real." Nicoll even admits that to the rational mind all this will seem absurd.

> Following the evidence of our senses we believe that the present exists, but that the past and the future are non-existent and incapable of existing. *Where could they exist*? In what room or space? ... To imagine that our present moment is only *one point* in an infinitely larger present seems absurd. (p. 79)

He points out that all our thoughts about the past are colored by a certain sense of unreality about anything that is "over and done with" – what he calls "was-ness" – and with that "was-ness" comes a kind of impatience and even sentimentality about the past. As long as we believe that only the present moment of life is actual and that all else is nonexistent or forever lost, then we are bound to have one particular and limited feeling of ourselves.

Nicoll continues this line of reasoning by pointing out that we are psychologically built around the natural belief in passing time, but that it might be better labeled "annihilating time." Once an event is over – even though there may still be longing or guilt or anger about what happened – there is still the sense that the moment is gone forever, that it is annihilated by the inexorable march of time and hence is no longer alive.

But a different understanding of time is possible to us, and Nicoll invites us to consider an ancient Hermetic teaching about time. It includes a meditative exercise designed to expand our consciousness about the nature of time. Successfully and repeatedly completed, it has the potential to open us in such a way that personal transformation becomes more readily possible. The exercise cryptically instructs the seeker to "expand ourselves to the magnitude of all existence. Only in this way can life become permanently unified." In other words, to reach a state of wholeness – a life that has become unified – a certain kind of expansion is required. Usually, though, we think of "expansion" in terms of increasing something about space, such as getting taller or wider. But these ancient teachings surprisingly inform us that it's an expansion in the dimensions of time that's required. It's a simultaneous remembering of one's life as a whole, the convergence of all the periods of a lifespan into the present moment.

In Nicoll's (and Ouspensky's) language it is the experience of a "higher space" in which space and time interact in such a way that we realize that all experiences in a lifespan have a living quality in the present moment. As Nicoll describes further the Hermetic exercise, he quotes the specific steps that one is to undertake. It's an imaginative, meditation process to feel how every point in one's biography is alive and present right now.

> What is "the magnitude of all existence"? The sense of existence throughout all one's Time is meant – the sense of this living "organism" in higher space ... [The Hermetic author writes], "*Think that you are not yet begotten, think that you are in the womb, that you are young, that you are old, that you are dead, that you are in the world beyond the grave. Grasp all that in your thought at once – all times and places.*" The perception of this idea – that the life is extended in time – is a step toward the unification of life. (Nicoll, *Living Time*, p. 101-102, quoting from *Hermetica*, edited and translated by Walter Scott, Oxford University Press, 1924, Vol. I., p. 221)

This exercise is not unlike my dream in which all my selves were converging in the forest. There is a simultaneous remembering of one's life as a whole. In essence, the Hermetic exercise serves to make the invisible aspects of life more present, alive, and real for us. As Nicoll continues to describe it:

> The Hermetic exercise is to produce background, through making the invisible side of things real. It is only through our conceptions of the invisible that we can change our present-moment psychology. As it is, everything that

> happens to us at the moment influences us. We have a momentary psychology, against which the Hermetic exercise is surely directed. I maintain that *this momentary psychology rests on the distinction made between was, is, and will be* – that is, on the belief in passing time which makes only the instant seem to be the site of life. The result is a point of reaction that is over-stressed and shifting, and *one that gives no starting point for unity or integration* – one, in fact, that could not possibly do so. (p. 104)

And as we do this, it makes two powerfully transformative processes possible. First it awakens you to the realization that *your future self already exists* in some way. That makes it possible for you to have a relationship with the self you are in the process of becoming. It is the person that you are in the midst of changing into being. That self is *already alive* in the bigger picture of things. What's more, you can have relationship to it, you can be influenced, guided, and supported by it.

Second, the ancient Hermetic exercise opens a door to the transformative power of *forgiveness*. If the "past" is still alive and something we can have a direct relationship with, then the meaning of forgiveness is seen in a new way. The capacity to have a *living* relationship with your past self opens the possibility of authentic forgiveness.

In effect, it's possible to "change the past," in a manner of speaking. Maybe forgiveness is more than just a change of attitude about something that happened long ago. Instead, there might be a profound kind of forgiveness in which our consciousness actually *experiences something different taking place in the past.* That is, healing forgiveness on a much more profound level. In the language of those who believe in reincarnation, it would be the transformation of our karma.

But these are deep mysteries, and this kind of transformative forgiveness and healing, doesn't come from any simple step-by-step methodology. The Hermetic exercise can begin to awaken you to the potentials, it can connect you with new feelings of yourself and allow you to start having a living relationship with your past, present, and future. But to sustain that kind of consciousness – to embark on the journey of personal transformation, healing, and forgiveness in a sustained way – one spiritual discipline is indispensable. That is meditation, the topic of our next chapter.

Chapter 4

Transformative Meditation

"I have discovered that all human evil comes from this,
man's being unable to sit quietly in a room."
Blaise Pascal (1623-1662)
French mathematician and philosopher

Meditation works best for people who are not results-oriented.

That rather startling statement is the essence of what can be said or written about meditation. It's the basic message about how meditation is linked to personal change and the journey of transformation. But it flies in the face of our modern thinking – about virtually anything. We want results. We want technologies that produce predictable effects. It seems to our modern minds that there should be specific techniques that can be followed and they should lead to reliable results.

However, meditation is about "giving of ourselves to God" rather than "getting for ourselves" – even though the "getting" could be about admirable qualities such as enlightenment, health, or wholeness. As long as the mind-set is about what one can get or achieve from meditation, then it's still an activity of the personality self – it's still just self-improvement change and not transformation. Only by dropping our obsessions with results (even our very subtle obsessions) can we really discover what meditation does "to us" as opposed to "for us."

This is a hard-sell, though. In the early 1970s meditation was "sold" to North Americans and Europeans as a dependable results-oriented technique to do all kinds of wonderful things: lower blood pressure, enhance emotional adjustment, and sharpen mental clarity. And, in fact, that sales-pitch continues today. But it misses the fundamental point of what meditation is all about. Seen more deeply we realize that meditation works best for those who are not so results-focused. Its transformative influence comes as a natural by-product of our *willingness* to be awakened and healed by the transformative powers of the universe – not by our *willfulness* and its drive to achieve impressive changes in ourselves. The point is this: The results that the personality's mind would imagine are unlikely to be the results that are most important to awakening and transformation. Or put another way, a conditioned, dysfunctional mind cannot heal itself, and the results that it would hope for are essentially more-of-the-same. Psychology and psychotherapy help us understand and accept our wounds; but it is meditation that transforms them.

A Brief Look at the Essence of Meditation

Although this is the shortest chapter in the book, in many ways it is the most significant. Nothing is more central than meditation – properly understood – to our capacity to truly change. In meditation, the factors that influence transformative change come into clear focus. It has been said that in the Orient, teachings begin with the most important point, and then everything else that follows is simply an elaboration. In essence that means starting with the "punch line" and then filling in the details. The Occidental way is the opposite: present all the details and build up to the punch line or conclusion. So, even though this approach from Western thinking is more familiar to us, let's approach meditation from the way it might be done in the East, starting with this principle:

Meditation is fundamentally letting go of
busyness so something new can grow in us.

That definition, short as it is, leaves lots of room for explanation and elaboration. But right off we can see two key phrases that stand at the heart of the matter: "letting go" and "busyness." The first refers to surrender and allowing. It affirms our innate capacity to drop something – a habit pattern, a compulsion, a worry, a fear, etc. Of course, that's no easy matter because we get quite attached to these products of the modern mind.

And then "busyness." Is there any word that better captures the flavor of modern life? How did we ever let ourselves get so busy? But the "busyness" named in this simple definition of meditation is not so much all the things we are trying to do in the course of a single day. Instead, it's a matter of what is going on in the mind – the way that we have cluttered our thinking and feeling to the point where we have no clarity or centeredness.

And so, meditation is letting go of busyness. It is surrendering the familiar workings of the mind that support a distorted, narrow picture of who we are.

The 11 Most Important Things to Remember About Meditation

1. Meditation creates space by emptying oneself of the personality. We have so little space – psychological space – in the way that we typically live. Whether it's the "busyness" referred to above or countless other ways that we clutter our lives (agendas, distractions, obligations, addictions), there are so many obstacles to transformative change. What's needed is a clearing and the creation of mental and emotional space in which something new can be created. The Buddha invites us to think about meditation in this way – the experience of emptiness or the void. Westerners tend to misinterpret and take this to imply some sort of nihilistic point of view. But that emptiness or space is a prerequisite for the rebirth of one's identity.

2. Meditation is a dance back and forth between the masculine and feminine. First the masculine principle is active with intention and discipline to simply show up for meditation, and then to put distractions aside to create an open space. Then the masculine (i.e., effort and striving) must *surrender* so the feminine principle can *create* in that spaciousness. It is like allowing oneself to become pregnant – inwardly. It creates the feeling, "Here am I, send me, use me." In that womb-like spaciousness a new sense of life emerges. Finally, as the meditation session ends, the dance concludes with the masculine stepping forward again, ready to apply in daily life what has been born in the spacious stillness.

3. Meditation is relaxation and rest. How unfamiliar is the sense of relaxation and genuine rest for modern men and women. We even end up working at being relaxed. We make it into a project, yet another accomplishment. And therefore, something like meditation, that promises to give us profound rest, ends up becoming yet another achievement that we strain to master.

Just imagine what might happen for us as meditators if we made this daily exercise simply something that would be fun and effortless. What if we could drop all feelings of strain and effort to be "good at it"? In other words, if we can let go of our expectations and hoped-for-results and simply be present during the meditation time, then its transformative power can start to work through us *in its own way.* What a relief to discover that you don't have to excel at meditation; you don't have to prove yourself. You can just relax, rest, and enjoy being present to yourself.

4. Meditation is the enhancement of awareness. Rather than fight with your body or mind, meditation is an opportunity just to be aware of what's happening in the present moment. A thought comes up; just be aware of it. Don't let it carry you off; don't be frustrated that your mind won't quiet down. Some place in your body feels uncomfortable; just be aware of it. Don't think that the distracting body sensation is preventing you from meditating; simply be aware of what the energy of your body is doing in the present moment.

Perhaps this all sounds too simple. Surely there is something more complicated and demanding about meditation than just being more aware. And yet, awareness itself is subtly difficult to achieve. We are constantly falling back asleep, constantly allowing the non-awareness and the habit patterns of the personality to take over.

5. Meditation is witnessing the witness. Through non-critical awareness, a witnessing consciousness begins to emerge. This "witnessing I," as Gurdjieff called it, is able to stand apart from all the busy-ness and obsessiveness of the personality self. But meditation takes things even one step deeper. A more profound kind of awareness begins to emerge – one in which something in us is even aware that this witnessing consciousness is quietly doing its work. As the meditation teacher Osho describes it:

> Start watching your thoughts but don't stop there. When thoughts have disappeared then don't think that you have arrived. One more thing has to be done, one more step. Now

watch the watcher. Now just witness the witnessing. Nothing else is left, only you are... By watching the mind, the mind disappears. By watching the witness, the witness expands and becomes universal. (*The Book of Wisdom*, p. 162)

6. Meditation is going beyond the judgments or questions-and-answers. Closely related to the principle of witnessing consciousness is the experience of dropping the judging mind. The rational mind of physical consciousness is constantly seeking distinctions. Just look at human philosophy over the ages. The intellect is mightily engaged in finding finer and finer distinctions of logic. Judgments are not only allowed, they are demanded. But at what price? What is it about ourselves that is lost in the machinations of a mind that compulsively judges every experience that comes along? Surely we lose something about our wholeness and the intuitive, spiritual side of ourselves. Meditation is a way to reclaim that aspect of ourselves which the judging mind cannot comprehend.

One immediate way in which we are challenged to practice this principle about meditation concerns our tendency to want meditation to be the source of answers to our questions. How easy it is to spend the fifteen or thirty minutes of a meditation session simply trying to get a new mental angle on the problems and worries of the day. And admittedly, we sometimes do seem to get fresh thoughts about our difficulties from such introspection. But was that meditation? Probably not.

Meditation takes us to a place beyond questions and answers, if we are willing to go there. The Truth doesn't come to us as an "answer." Instead, it comes when we are open and spacious and willing. It comes when we have dropped the questions – when we have allowed ourselves to be in a state of unquestioning awareness.

7. Meditation involves using the mind – not being used *by* the mind. This is a subtle distinction, but crucial. Many of the principles listed above seem to have a derogatory attitude toward the mind, in effect making it the jailer of our imprisoned soul-self. And no doubt there is much about how the mind tends to operate which actually does keep us stuck and which resists any sort of genuine transformation.

But at the same time, the mind is an invaluable part of the

human soul. It is the creator of our human experience. It is the builder of our reality. It is even the bridge between the spirit and the body, if it is used properly. Yet, in spite of the fabulous potentials, the mind ends up using us, rather than us using it. Our spirit becomes the slave of the conditioned, habitual mind.

So, what is to be done, and what role can meditation play? Simply this: Meditation is an invitation to experience ourselves as no-mind, so that we can then pick the mind back up and use it creatively to bring health and peace and joy into our own lives and the lives of those around us. But unless the human spirit and will can experience itself even briefly through no-mind, then we are endlessly caught in the illusions and delusions that are foisted on us by the wounds and conditioning of the personality's mind.

8. Meditation is deepening trust in yourself and your roots. Most fundamentally, our childhood conditioning was to not trust ourselves – to mistrust our own instincts, our own bodies, and our own longings. We were told what we ought to do, what we ought to believe, and who we ought to be. Instilled deeply in all of us – even those who seemingly had a "nice childhood" – was the lesson of self-mistrust.

And so, an important aspect of meditation is experimenting with how it feels to regain trust for one's own energy and one's own calling in life. All kinds of worries and "voices" (audible or not) are likely to arise as soon as we begin to reestablish contact with ourselves in this way. That resistance, stored deeply in the subconscious mind, is a potent force that runs counter to meditation.

But with the patient and consistent practice of meditation, much of that resistance can begin to melt. And with the loosening of the hold of mistrust, we start to embrace ourselves as we are, not as anyone else told us we ought to be. With that kind of self-trust can come an even deeper kind of trust: trust in the unknown. For meditation to be genuinely deep and transformative we have to be willing to go into the unknown and to trust the invisible forces that can guide our unfoldment.

9. Meditation is dropping your beliefs so that you can come to know. The essence of meditation is to directly experience the Truth – about ourselves and the universe. Ironically, it is our beliefs that often get in the way of that encounter. Our cherished assumptions and dogmas about how life works need to be dropped, and meditation is one place where this can happen.

In a sense, "believers" always remain childish, immature. They assume that they already have the truth, and so no genuine inquiry is necessary. The Truth is expected to adjust to fit them. "Believers" don't change and grow. "Already having the answers," they have become a closed system unto themselves or unto their group that has the same beliefs.

But meditation involves opening ourselves to growth and change; it means becoming an open system. Meditation is a way of adjusting ourselves to fit the Truth, not the other way around. And that can be scary because we find great comfort in our beliefs. They have given us a measure of safety, but at a great cost. Meditation is courageously taking the risk to say, "I really don't know yet," and to be open to what can come.

10. Meditation is possible only with commitment and zest. Dedicated enthusiasm may well be as important to meditation as anything else. The steady willingness to be persistent with daily meditation is what's needed. To again quote the meditation teacher Osho:

> People have forgotten the language of commitment, involvement. People don't know the beauties of commitment, they don't know the joys of dedication. They don't know what it means to be utterly dedicated to something. To be utterly dedicated to something means giving birth to a soul in you. It integrates you, it gives you a backbone. Otherwise people who don't have any experience of commitment – in love, in trust – they live a life without a spine...Millions of people in the world remain immature, childish, for the simple reason that they don't know how to commit themselves. They just remain rootless. (*The Book of Wisdom*, p.110)

But commitment needs to be nourished by enthusiasm and zest. There needs to be *feeling* behind the commitment if it has any chance to be sustained. When you have zest for life, then you can look forward to each meditation session – in fact, look forward to whatever life will bring you today.

11. Meditation is dropping the sense of passing time. As we saw in Chapter 3, the alteration of our sense of time is important for the transformation process. As long as we are stuck in the perception of time as one-dimensional – linear, passing time – then the personality self holds sway over us. In a sense, the conditioned "mind" that is so familiar to daily living *is* time. To make this principle a little more practical, consider this: the mind of your personality self almost never dwells on the present moment. It is concerned with the remembered past and with an imagined future. The conditioned mind is always inclined to drift away from what is, right now.

Through meditation the experience of time is transformed. We begin to experience the sense of eternity that vertically cuts through each and every moment along a horizontal timeline. Through meditation we begin to experience a second dimension of time that opens our awareness to the rhythmic, cyclical qualities of how life meets us. And going deeper, meditation transforms time into even a third realm, making possible the feeling of a spiral – that time not only turns back on itself to connect past-present-future, but it also unfolds purposefully, with countless possibilities.

A Starting Place for Finding Your Own Method

You may still wonder, "What's a direct way in which I can get started with meditation?" Perhaps the simplest starting point is a meditative technique that focuses attention on your breathing. But the transformation power of this or any method depends upon a proper attitude toward the practice. Remember the principle with which this chapter began: Meditation works best for people who are not results-oriented. If you can embrace the attitude outlined in the ten principles described in the previous section, then meditation can begin to do its work on you.

Practice even for just five or ten minutes a day the following three-part meditation procedure. Regularity – preferably on a daily basis at about the same time – works best. Sitting comfortably, you can do whatever helps to get into a centered, purposeful frame of mind: listening to soothing or inspiring music for a few minutes, reading from sacred literature, or taking a few moments for prayer, either aloud or silent. Sit comfortably in a chair, which keeps your back reasonably erect. Pick a setting, which is quiet so that your attention won't be distracted by outside disturbances.

The first part of the meditative procedure is breath attention. With your eyes closed, move your attention gently to your breathing. You need not try to control the rate of the depth of your breathing, but simply keep your attention on the flowing in and out of each breathing cycle.

Practice this technique, and you shall quickly see how it demands the conscious presence of will. How easily attention becomes undirected and is captured by distractions. You may find it helpful to count breaths silently as an aid to keeping your focus. Or you may prefer to hold the attitude described by Lama Anagarike Govinda in his book *Creative Meditation and Multi-Dimensional Experience:*

> Thus we experience the very nature of life by surrendering ourselves to (breathing's) rhythm, instead of interfering with it, because it is the rhythm of the universe that breathes through us. Instead of thinking ourselves as the agents and originators of this movement ("I am breathing in; I am breathing out," etc.), we should rather feel "the universe breathes in me, streams through me: it is not I who is breathing, but the universe through me." (p. 119).

Of course, meditation can and should be viewed as something more profound than just sitting for five minutes and observing the breath. As a second step, use your will to keep attention on your highest spiritual aspiration. A mantra or affirmation is a good way to keep focused. It provides a centering point for the will. The words you choose should have a powerful, evocative quality – they need to be able to awaken strong feelings for the spiritual ideal. Consider one example of an affirmation: if you had chosen "Love" as your spiritual ideal, an appropriate affirmation for meditation might be something such as "Let me always be a channel of blessings and love to others."

The affirmation becomes a focal point of attention during the silence of meditation. The affirmation or mantra is essentially a "tool," something to begin to quiet and focus the mind – so that you can begin to use it rather than it using you.

What words should you choose for your affirmation? Other than writing your own, you might take a favorite line from the Bible (e.g., "Be still and know that I am God") or from other sacred scripture. Some meditators keep their affirmations quite brief and, in fact, use only the short phrase they have selected for their spiritual ideal.

You may find it helpful to create in your mind some visual imagery that relates to your affirmation and helps you get in touch with it. For example, some meditators find it helpful to imagine themselves sitting in a special spiritual place. The image of that setting then allows them to identify more quickly with the life purpose that the affirmation represents.

As you center your mind and move into the quiet of meditation, focus your attention on the words of the affirmation and any images you're using. Do this until you begin to experience the feeling and spirit behind the words. You are using your conscious will to concentrate and keep your attention one-pointed. However, the effort you make to direct attention is not an intellectual effort to dissect the affirmation or analyze the images. Instead, let your attention rest upon the *feeling and spirit* the affirmation begins to call forth from your unconscious mind. This stage may require much practice because of the strong tendency for your attention to drift off to distracting thoughts and emotions.

Once you have reached a point where you recognize that the affirmation has begun to do its work – that new feelings are being awakened – then *drop the words and any images you have created.* This is the silence of meditation. Here you rest in silent attention in the quiet spirit of the ideal your affirmation represents. At this point, words are unnecessary. They have done their job by getting you back in touch with another way of feeling and seeing yourself and life.

When your attention drifts, repeat the steps of focusing attention on the words, then let go of them once you have their spirit. In other words, you can expect that your capacity to stay in the silence will be limited. At first, you will probably find that after just ten or fifteen seconds of silently holding the feeling of your affirmation a distracting thought or emotion will grab your attention and pull you away. When you recognize you have been caught up in a distraction, go back to focusing on the affirmation until you re-experience its meaning and spirit. You may have to repeat this sequence many times in a single meditation session. Even experienced meditators have to go back frequently and reawaken to their sense of highest purpose by recalling the affirmation and then re-attaining the silence.

Finally you come to a third phase of this three-step approach. Just let go. *Surrender all efforts to make something happen.* Let go of any compulsion to be results-oriented. All the previous steps have included effort on your part to direct the meditation session. Even if you have no expectations or desires for some special experience in meditation, conscious effort and the exercise of will have been necessary. However, the last phase of your meditation should include a short period during which you fully surrender, discontinuing all conscious effort. When you have spent sufficient time holding in silent attention the feeling and meaning of your affirmation, and you feel permeated by its spirit, *release even the affirmation.* Drop it all – your beliefs, your expectations, your hopes.

A good way to experience the surrender is to refocus your attention on your breathing. In other words, once you have let the meaning of your affirmation permeate both your conscious and unconscious, then spend several minutes in attentive breathing. This exercise at the close is not to force a change in consciousness by an extraordinary breathing technique. Instead, by letting your attention focus on something as simple as your breath, the power of what you have subconsciously achieved in the previous steps is able to touch you even more deeply.

The key to this final step is the word "surrender." There must be a sense of giving up (but not of "giving in") – letting go of all mental efforts to force something to happen.

Part III:

THE HUMAN WILL AS THE KEY TO SOUL TRANSFORMATION

Chapter 5

What is Free Will?

Your will – the key to change and transformation – is the greatest mystery of modern times. But it's not the kind of mystery that is solved by playing detective and gathering facts. Instead, it is a deeper kind of mystery that rests in the very heart of your existence. If you experience the meaning and power of your will, then you know yourself in a whole new way. You will have found one of the basic ingredients of your soul. And you will have found the part of your soul that makes growth and transformation possible.

Certainly there are other great mysteries in addition to the will. The human mind is one. Especially in the past one hundred years there have been remarkable discoveries about the extraordinary realms of the unconscious mind. Research into meditation, hypnosis, dreams, and ESP has demonstrated previously unbelievable capacities of the mind – all of them relevant, too, for the transformation process. But it is the mystery of the will that should now gain our attention. All those tremendous features of the mind have meaning only if the will is healthy and alive – able to direct us along an authentic path of soul transformation.

What, in essence, is this mysterious principle we call the will? Even if we cannot fully explain it, we can still ask about *the features it brings to living* and about how it helps establish profound meaning in our lives.

The role of the will is among the most fundamental questions in contemporary spirituality. In many ways the so-called "consciousness movement" or "new religions" have failed to provide to people in our society what they have promised. Certainly the failure may be largely on the part of the people rather than the teachings. On the one hand, we have an array of remarkable tools available to the contemporary seeker: insights and techniques ranging from meditation to reincarnation, from telepathy to biofeedback. Except for a few pockets of impressive change, why hasn't our culture been transformed? We have discovered the reality of psychosomatic health, the power of the mind to heal. Why are there so many sick people in our society? We have discovered the underlying oneness of all mind. Why is there still so much discord and animosity? We have discovered the inherent connections between human consciousness and the planet Earth. Why is there still pollution and disregard for the environment?

Perhaps what has been missing is a sensitive, honest encounter with this forgotten mystery of human experience: the will. For all our scientific, psychological, and metaphysical achievements in the past two generations, we still seem to be rather powerless to bring about the kinds of changes in the world which are possible. The next great frontier for us is not in the realm of physical science, mental exploration, or philosophical speculation. The cutting edge of contemporary spirituality is our encounter with this profound mystery of the human will. If we become initiates of this mystery, it shall provide us with the inner power to achieve all of the possibilities for ourselves and for our world which we can envision, yet have seemed helplessly unable to manifest.

What is the will? Is it a particular state of mind? Is it a certain kind of energy? Or is it instead one of the basic building blocks of human experience, something on an equal footing with mind and energy itself? Perhaps the mystery and the power of the will is best understood by treating it as philosophers would a fundamental "category" of human life – that is to say, the will can be seen as something so basic to who we are that it cannot be explained in terms of other essential building blocks such as energy and mind.

By way of analogy, we might think of color. There are three primary pigments: red, blue, and yellow. These are the basic building blocks of other colors. The color green can be explained in terms of the interaction of two other primary colors: yellow and blue. The color purple, by the interaction of red and blue. But how can blueness be explained? It is not a specialized form of red or yellow, nor can it be created by a specialized mixing of these other two primary colors. Blue itself is one of the fundamental building blocks.

In a similar fashion, we can think of the will as a basic category of life, one of life's fundamental "colors." Will cannot be explained as a kind of energy nor as a particular state of mind. Life can be understood and given meaning only as we are able to see and relate to will as an independent faculty or ingredient of the soul on an equal footing with energy and mind.

We might go further and say that will is that which makes us nonmachine-like. We can never build a machine-like model of life that fully includes the impact of will because the will is not of that realm or order. Certainly, we can try to build models or analogies which help us understand how the will operates, but any such effort will have a limitation. The will introduces into human experience something that cannot be reduced to mechanistic formulas. If we were made up merely of energy and mind, then highly sophisticated flowcharts might be able to account for all human experience. If we were made up of mind and energy alone, then we might foresee a time in the future when highly advanced computers could fully simulate human consciousness. But the will, as one of the three fundamental ingredients of the human soul (along with mind and life energy or spirit), makes machine-like replication impossible.

A Historical Review

Today in our personal lives and in the world we face crises that can be traced back directly to a failure of the human will. Our very need to change and transform is largely because of a failure of will. Yet our inability to understand and appreciate the will is not due to the lack of efforts in history to study this problem. Despite an overall tendency to ignore or discount the will, there have always been those (from ancient times even to the present) who have made an effort to understand its power and significance. Despite the fact that most thinkers in philosophy, psychology, and social and medical sciences still have little appreciation for the will, there is a long tradition about this topic. Over the centuries we see a sequence of questions and possible answers about the will being formulated, and it is this same sequence that each of us may go through in a personal encounter with the mystery and power of will as we seek transformation.

The historical development of understanding centers around three questions, which can be posed first in philosophical language and then in more practical daily language.

1. Are we "free" or is life predestined?
2. What is it that connects thought and action?
3. Is there a faculty of the soul that stands opposite the impulses coming from the physical senses?

All three of these questions sound very intellectual, and yet they are questions that you may ask yourself in daily living in different forms. For example, you may find yourself wondering about the nature of freedom. To what extent is your life free? How much are you controlled by the patterns of living you learned from your parents and school teachers, or by the constraints placed upon you by the government and community in which you live? How much was your life predetermined at birth by your genetic makeup, which largely shaped your physical appearance and intelligence? Can you really say that you are free?

Or, why do you so often fail to do what you think you ought to do? Why do you often have the best of intentions and yet no physical actions or results come out of it? What are the mysterious connections that allow your thinking process to be translated into practical application?

Or, what keeps you from living your life totally by impulse? What keeps you from being merely a machine that reacts to life? What inward faculty allows you to choose and respond in your own best interest to physical stimuli and appetites? The answer to this and all of these questions rests with the nature of your will.

To study the way in which theologians, philosophers, and psychologists have for centuries wrestled with these kinds of questions leaves us with a difficulty in terminology. For example, we must ask whether or not ancient and modern thinkers used similar words to mean the same thing. Do terms such as "spirit," "will," and "reason" mean the same today that they meant hundreds of years ago? Can we even translate into modern language what they were writing about in their own language? Furthermore, in any careful historical study, a whole array of related terms is also introduced – concepts such as wish, choice, purpose, impulse, appetite, and desire. In fact, another entire book would be required to summarize adequately the centuries of theories and argumentation on these questions about human experience. This chapter, however, is about a modern theory of the meaning of will, and the paradoxical role it plays in personal transformation.

Where do we begin in formulating a modern theory of the importance of the will? Some of the most influential thinkers of the 19th and 20th centuries don't provide support. For example, Charles Darwin and those evolutionists who followed him have little place for the human will in their theories. For them, the principal agent of change in the development of humanity is not the will but, instead, genetic chemistry and the forces of the environment. Sigmund Freud in his psychoanalytic theories proposed that will is illusory, that the principal determining agent in our lives is a kind of primal impetus from the unconscious that he called the libido. Neither of these two great pillars of modern Western thought leaves much room for a human faculty such as will.

One notable exception is the American philosopher and psychologist, William James, who wrote in the late 19th and early 20th centuries. James' ideas are a good starting point for a modern theory of will. His work has never been as popular as that of Freud, yet perhaps in the future he will be rediscovered and reappreciated. James went through long periods of extraordinary self-questioning – almost to the point of being self-destructive – concerning the question of personal freedom. Finally, he arrived at a conclusion (described in his diary on April 30, 1870) of assuming that free will *does* exist. For him, the first act of that free will was to assert its reality and to live life as if he had a self-determining agent within called will.

> I think that yesterday was a crisis in my life. I finished the first part of Renouvier's "Essais" and see no reason why his definition of Free Will – the sustaining of a thought *because I choose* to when I might have other thoughts – need be the definition of an illusion. At any rate, I will assume for the present – until next year – that it is no illusion. *My first act of free will shall be to believe in free will.* [Emphasis added]

Much of James' writing about the nature of will focuses on concerns about how it operates to create physical actions. How does the will help you move from the idea of doing something to the act of doing it? In his theory, the will draws upon the memory of previous physical movements. We are able to re-create voluntarily and freely those physical movements because we can select memory patterns of the *sensations* created by those movements when they were completed in the past. You can choose to move your left arm because your will draws upon memories of how it felt in the past when you moved it. Of course, this notion creates a sort of "which came first, the chicken or the egg" dilemma. James proposed that any movement was first produced in a reflexive or accidental way and only then, by drawing upon the memory of it, could we voluntarily re-create actions with the will.

This principle of "Idea-motor-action" and the related concept of "kinaesthetic image" make for a rather complicated theory that need not concern us here. What we do want to appreciate from William James' writings and come back to later are two key principles. First is the way in which the will is related to imagination. One of the ways in which we experience the workings of the will is through *its capacity to function imaginatively.* Your will can activate the imaginative function of your mind. It can stimulate imagination to draw upon memories of the feelings and sensations of the past. It works with body memories and the memories of thoughts and feelings. In other words, your will can direct the realm of your attitudes and emotions, *if you use it.* Through an act of will, you can create certain thoughts and feelings because you are able to draw imaginatively on memories of similar thoughts and feelings from the past.

There is a second key principle on which we can begin to build a modern theory of the will. James recognized that the fundamental faculty of the will is *a capacity to direct our attention.* The will allows us to put attention upon certain patterns of mind and not upon others. We have both an inner life and an outer life that go in particular directions fundamentally because the will can place attention on certain imaginings or mind patterns instead of upon others. If you wish to feel the reality of your own will in this very moment, experience the way in which you have the capacity to move your attention. Right now, put your attention on the color of this page of paper. Then move your attention to the top of your head. Finally move it to the memory of what you ate at your last meal. Your ability to do that simple, three-part exercise is evidence of your will in action.

We can build upon these two fundamental insights offered by James. Even though he was a pioneer in a modern appreciation for the human will, much more can be added. Next we will examine a broader picture of the nature of will. A new understanding is needed about this key ingredient which stands as a centerpiece of transformative change.

A New Understanding of the Will

The time is ripe for a new understanding of the will, one that emphasizes its role as the essential ingredient of personal transformation. Of course, not everyone may agree, because some see no need for such a thing. For example, in modern psychology, where the behavioristic and psychoanalytic approaches predominate, there is no room for something like the will being a responsible director and shaper of our lives. But it is a hopeful sign that in recent decades a developing new position in psychology does appreciate the significance of the will. Many of the leading thinkers in both humanistic and transpersonal psychology have placed the will at the center of growth and development. In addition, the scientific study of biofeedback – i.e., the voluntary control of internal physical states – has begun to develop scientific credibility.

How can we move from these hopeful signs to a truly comprehensive picture of what the will is and what it can do in our lives? A good place to start is a multifaceted definition that shows the richness and the depth of meaning inherent in the human will. At least nine features should be a part of this new understanding.

1. Active Principle

What can we call the will? Do we speak of it as a type of energy or as a state of mind? Or do we give the will equal status with pure energy as well as with the mind? To give the will that recognition, we need to select a label which stresses its independent status. Perhaps the best wording is the phrase "an active principle within the soul." That is to say, it is a faculty inherent in the soul's nature. Furthermore, it is a principle that is active, that is dynamic and that participates in the soul's growth, transformation, and evolution.

Let's make this abstract notion more practical with a simple example. Suppose you suddenly remember that the day after tomorrow is your uncle's birthday. Should you take the time and effort to send a card? What other obligations do you face today and how high a priority is it to keep your uncle happy? Suppose you decide to purchase and mail a card today. The remembrance of his birthday and the analysis of whether or not to send a card are both functions of your mind. But the decision in favor of sending a card and the behaviors needed to make that happen both fall in the realm of your will – an active principle.

2. Individualizer

The will is that which makes each of us an individual creation – it is that which makes each of us a unique spiritual being. If we use the concept that "mind is the builder and creator of our life experience," then in a complementary fashion we could say that "will is the individualizer that allows us to feel our unique identity."

But how is it that the will creates uniqueness and individuality? Is it analogous to the serial number on a television set or on the engine block of an automobile? No, because what makes us unique is not so much a specialized imprint as it is an active principle that allows us to be self- reflective or self-aware. The will is the individualizer because it allows us to know ourselves as ourselves. The hallmark of a being with a will is *self-reflection.*

Of course, we do not always live our lives with this kind of self reflectiveness. Rarely do we take time to step outside ourselves and see ourselves objectively. For this reason, we can say that most often the will is asleep within us. It is unconscious – an untapped potential. But if the will awakens, then this kind of self-awareness leads to an awakening of true individuality.

3. Chooser

This is the faculty of will with which we are most familiar. The will allows us to make choices among alternative courses of action. However, the choosing process relates not just to physical behaviors but more fundamentally to the way in which we choose *to direct attention*. Recall that for William James this capacity to place attention in one direction instead of another is the fundamental way by which we experience the reality of will. Oftentimes our "choices" to act in certain ways are really quite predetermined by the way in which we have chosen to place our attention in the inner world of thought and feeling.

4. Agent of Obedience

Not only does the will allow each of us to chart a self-determined course for life, it also allows us to be subservient to or obedient to influences which come from beyond our personal sense of identity. Every system of personal transformation states that enlightenment requires of us a cooperative relationship with influences bigger than ourselves. It is this feature of will which counterbalances the preceding one which emphasizes self-determination and personal choice. This is the paradox of power. The will empowers us to choose freely and determine our own life direction. But simultaneously the will offers us another option: to be empowered by something Greater through an obedient *willingness*. The will allows forces and influences from beyond the personal sphere to motivate and shape our lives. Although the word "obedience" is not a popular one, it is an essential requirement for the path of soul.

5. Changer

The will allows us to reshape our lives, even though we already have strong habits and tendencies. For every individual there is a certain momentum to life which, if allowed to play itself out, would result in very predictable outcomes. However, through the will we can change those patterns. Some philosophies about the will even go so far as to say that every condition based upon our past can be altered by the will.

However, when we can claim this potential for change, we must combine it with a sense of patience. The capacity to change patterns does not always mean that the change can be accomplished immediately. Much of the misunderstanding and misrepresentation of the will has been a distortion of this particular attribute. Yes, we can change things in our lives but, if we attempt it with impatience, then it frequently leads to unhappy conclusions.

6. Opposer of Mind.

The most intriguing feature of the will is that it stands in opposition to mind. The significance of this principle should not be underestimated. There are ways in which we frequently experience how the will opposes a *tendency* of the mind. For example, the mind tells us that it wants an extra piece of dessert and the will may play a role to oppose or oppress that desire pattern. Or, another example: the mind wants to play and replay thoughts of self-pity, but the will may intervene to oppose this tendency by giving attention to a more cheerful outlook.

7. Developer

The will stands at the heart of the soul's spiritual development. Through the way in which the will is applied, the result is either evolution or "de-evolution" – either soul development or soul retrogression. Why is the will so central to soul development? Simply because the goal of soul development is to fully know our own individuality, yet simultaneously to be one with the whole of life. The will individualizes us and allows us to have this self-reflective knowledge of ourselves. So its proper use is an essential requirement of spiritual transformation. In addition, the will can foster oneness. As the personal will is brought into harmony with the divine will, the experience of oneness with God is made possible.

8. Motivator

The will gets us moving in life. Mind can provide for us a pattern of thinking, feeling, or acting; but unless there is an impetus initiated by the will toward action, there are never results. A person in whom the will is slumbering is a person of little motivation, a person who is indifferent. Yet, when that same person learns to awaken and train the will, the possibilities for action and change come alive.

9. Guide

The will can guide the mind. If "mind is the builder," we might well ask, "But what is it that directs or guides that building process?" In other words, if the functionings of mind can be symbolized by a builder or carpenter, we should wonder what it is that serves as the foreman or even the architect of this building job. If the will is asleep, then this building proceeds in a haphazard fashion and each carpenter on the job may be building what he thinks the finished product ought to look like, only to discover that the results are unusable. However, as a kind of hidden soul power, we have the potential within us to shape our lives. The will can guide and direct the creative workings of the mind.

In summary, we have nine key ingredients which begin to formulate a new understanding of the human will. As we expand our picture of the will and how it operates transformationally in our lives, we can build on these fundamental characteristics:

- active principle
- individualizer
- chooser
- agent of obedience
- changer
- opposer of mind
- developer
- motivator
- guide

The Slumbering Seed of Your Future

Let's return to the most intriguing feature in this new understanding of will – its opposition to mind. Our life experience is a byproduct of the creative tension between these two elements of the soul. *Consciousness is an interplay of mental images and will.* Mental images are principally associated with our past. This makes sense if we think back to the concept that mind is the builder. In other words, the mind is an active force within us that can give a pattern or shape to the life force which we call spirit. When the mind works with pure creative energy to give it a pattern, that mental image continues to have existence long after its creation. We've all heard the phrase "thoughts are things." It simply means that once the mind has built something through its attitudes or emotions, what it has created continues over time. The products of the mind live on.

We might go so far as to make this claim, which at first may sound ridiculous:

Anything which appears as an "image" or a "form" really belongs to the past.

What are examples of the images and forms referred to in this statement? Your dream images. The form of your physical body. Mental images that pop into your mind from familiar attitudes and emotions. Anything that you can see in the material world. All of these are images and forms. As incredible as it may sound, they are all a reflection of something built by someone's mind *in the past*.

In contrast to the past orientation of mental images, the will is like a seed – it is of your future. The will draws you toward that which you are to become. The will is the principal agent of spiritual transformation. But which is more real – mental images or will? Which of the two gives you the best sense of who you really are? Clearly the answer is will.

The greatest mistake we can make is to identify our sense of personal identity with mental images. We hinder our own spiritual development when we identify ourselves with the past instead of with the seed of what we are evolving toward. The will has a kind of evolutionary wisdom. It is not the kind of repressive will that we would use to keep from eating an extra dessert, but a deeper will that is usually sleeping within us – a will toward enlightenment. This sleeping, unconscious will provides an impetus from deep within us toward wholeness.

However, what about the other, more familiar side of the coin – the conscious will? We cannot ignore the significance of conscious will and its proper use. But it can be understood, trained, and properly developed only if we see a bigger picture. The conscious will must come to reflect the deeper, wiser will.

If it is unconscious, how can we hope to experience it? One way is through true imagination. Imagination can reveal to us the direction toward our future, *the way* along which the will attempts to lead us. Something within us resonates strongly to or is sympathetic with this seed of our future. Out of this kind of soul level sympathy can arise truly imaginative insight and experience. Here imagination does not mean a re-experiencing of memories from our past. It's not saying to ourselves, "I imagined I was back in my third grade classroom." Instead it is imagination which is visionary, often having an element of surprise or wonder to it. It is will – directed imagination which transforms us to a future which is fresh and new.

In addition to imagination, there is a second way in which we can experience the workings of this deepest will of the soul. It involves a great sensitivity to the *feeling level* of human experience. Here we must see that there are three levels of activity within us – levels that were proposed by the Austrian-born spiritual philosopher Rudolf Steiner, whose ideas we examined in Chapter 1. The first is "thinking," a function which is relatively awake and immediately accessible for us. The second function is "feeling," which for us is not so much awake but instead analogous to dream-like experiences; that is to say, feeling is a way by which we can know things but which hasn't fully awakened within us, and it is usually dimly perceived – just as our dreaming experiences are usually not as direct and conscious as our waking ones.

The third function is, of course, "willing." Our experience of the genuine will of the soul, or our lack of experience of it, is analogous to sleep. To repeat: We are fully awake as thinking beings, we only perceive or know in a hazy dreamlike fashion through our feeling function, and we are usually asleep in relationship to the real willing of the soul.

However, because feeling occupies a role between thinking and willing, it provides an indirect way in which we can experience the real will of the soul. Often, by paying careful attention to the feelings which arise within us, we can learn the nature of this deeper sleeping faculty. Through nurturing the feeling side of ourselves, we can discover something about the nature of this seed within us, this great impetus toward our soul's destiny. We should keep in mind, however, that the term "feeling" describes something more subtle than emotions.

Often our emotions are mental images which draw our attention to the past – even urging us to repeat the past. In contrast to this, an experience of our feelings gives us a way of knowing (usually a "knowing without knowing how").

What does our feeling nature perceive? If it is not emotions (which belong more to the mental images we have built in the past), then what is it? Perhaps this "knowing through feeling" comes from a sensitivity to the deep, unconscious will of the soul. Will allows us to feel finer influences reaching us from a higher level. In contrast, our lives are usually directed and shaped by influences arising from the physical world of cause and effect. Our tendency is to be buffeted about by life, merely reacting to outside, material forces. In this familiar state, the will is not operative and we are asleep – spiritually "asleep." Although we walk around through life with our eyes open, a more realistic analysis of our human condition is that we are asleep to our real nature. We don't feel influences coming to us from a higher realm.

Personality and Individuality

As noted in Chapter 2, usually we live solely from that part of ourselves best described as "personality." The personality is a collection of habitual ways of thinking and feeling and acting. To a large extent it has been learned – taken on through imitation from those around us. This learning certainly begins in earliest childhood but continues through our adult years. The personality is not our real self. There is instead something deeper within us, what we might call "individuality" or the "Real I." It is our true identity – the soul or spiritual being.

The personality itself is not a single identity, and herein lies a great problem for us. The personality is made up of a collection of separate "I's" or subpersonalities. Each "I" is a distinct identity or role into which we fall from time to time.

For example, Janet is a 45-year-old businesswoman and mother of three children, ages 20, 14, and 9. In the course of a typical day her sense of personal identity shifts many times. She acts out many different roles as conditions around her change. By carefully observing her, we would come to see these distinct "I's" within her, and we might label each one. One "Janet" is the subpersonality she identifies with whenever she and her husband are getting along well – "the content wife." Another "Janet" is the tense, anxious "I" who often interacts with her 20-year-old son as the "worried mother." A quite different "Janet" is the "mellow mother" who has a relaxed relationship with her 9-year-old daughter.

At the office there are many different Janet subpersonalities: "the supportive boss," "the frazzled executive," and "the optimistic planner." In fact, dozens of different personality "I's" make up this collection which friends, family, and co-workers call "Janet." But at the level of personality, she is not a single identity.

For Janet, and for each of us, an ever-repeating shift from one "I" to another keeps us from a consistent sense of who we are. As forces and influences from material life nudge or push us toward identifying with a particular subpersonality "I," we forget the existence of other "I's." In actuality we live our lives with a multitude of "I's"; however, we like to pretend that we have a consistent identity.

Each subpersonality "I" has associated with it a set of habit patterns. These mechanical, automatic ways of thinking, feeling, and acting create a certain character for each subpersonality. Each subpersonality has its own agenda of desires and intentions, and in this fashion we might say that each has a "will of its own." In other words, what is commonly called "will" is in truth just one of these personality wills or at best a compromise among the diverse wills of many different subpersonality "I's."

However, this is not the authentic, deeper will of the soul. This is not what we can label "Real Will." Real Will is that which sensitizes us to influences that arise from outside of material laws of cause and effect. What are these higher influences? They are the forces of life which help us to synthesize, to be courageous and creative, and to provide meaningful solutions to life's problems. Real Will allows us to recognize new possibilities in situations where we have seen only a dilemma. It has a quality of patience and receptivity to it, since it requires us to be receptive to these influences which come from a higher level.

As the spiritual teacher, P.D. Ouspensky, once said: "Real Will is like suddenly seeing the solution to a mathematical problem." Haven't we all had that experience in life, where a new possibility or solution is suddenly presented to our minds? It usually comes after a period of intense work with the intellectual mind and effort with the conscious will. Yet the eventual solution comes to us as a gift, as we are open and receptive to its direction. This notion of Real Will is quite different from the traditional view of will which negates, suppresses, or attempts to force an issue. Maurice Nicoll wrote these words about the will as presented by his two teachers, P.D. Ouspensky and G.I. Gurdjieff:

> Mr. 0. [i.e., Ouspensky] refers to a different idea of will. It is something that finds right solutions. It unites separate things, it arranges in right order, and so creates something new. It contains the idea of new possibilities. It has to do with a certainty that a solution is possible, and with a certain kind of active patience towards the at-present unsolved situation, where one does not as yet see the next connection . . . G [i.e., Gurdjieff] once said that "patience is the Mother of Will." There is some solution. There is some possibility ... Out of every situation it is possible to get meaning. Things apparently diverse can he brought into some unity of meaning. It is like asking and waiting. (*Psychological Commentaries on the Teachings of Gurdjieff and Ouspensky*, p. 482)

A Parable of the Will

Sometimes a story or parable is helpful in understanding a complex subject. One of the best examples of a teaching parable about the will comes from Gurdjieff. This story is the Parable of the Horse, Carriage, and Driver.

In this allegory, which depicts the inner human state, we are shown how three levels – body, emotion, and intellect – are not in right relationship to one another. The parable begins by supposing that the driver of a horse and carriage has abandoned and forgotten his duties.

He is drunk in a public bar, wasting his money, and in his drunkenness he thinks that his status is that of a master instead of a servant. The horse is unfed and weakening, and its reins are in disarray or lost. The carriage has fallen into poor condition. The master is away from the scene and will not return to ride in the carriage until the driver is back on the box of the carriage and everything is in order.

In this parable the carriage represents the human body, the horse represents the emotions, and the driver, the intellectual mind. The state of drunkenness depicts the typical condition of our human minds. It stands for a kind of imagining which is based upon the past, the constant flow of mental images from our past with which we so readily identify. In our own "drunkenness" we mechanically shift from one subpersonality to the next, reacting to influences from material life. We are under the illusion that we are masters of ourselves and of our destiny, when in fact these three essential levels of our being are not at all in harmonious relationship to one another. Body, emotion, and intellect are not synchronized.

According to this parable, what must happen? First, the driver must awaken to understand his state. He must stop his drunken imaginings and momentarily dis-identify from his familiar state of mind long enough to recognize the condition into which he has fallen. Then, he must leave the public drinking house and go out and repair the carriage (i.e., care for his physical body) and attend to the needs of the horse (i.e., the emotional self). Once this is done the driver can lift himself up onto the box. Then, he can regain the reins and hold them firmly in hand. It is only at this point that the master can return to the scene and occupy his position within the carriage; it is only when the driver has done everything he can to set things in proper order that the master can come back. However, in this parable the master does not immediately give directions for proceeding. The driver must begin the movement of horse and carriage in the direction that he thinks best and then listen intently for corrective guidance from the master within the carriage.

This is a parable of extraordinary depth and insight for us, and it illustrates a number of places in which the human will plays a critical role. The will is an indispensable agent in that awakening which initiates a transformation in conditions. It is the will which directs attention and allows certain thoughts and emotions to shape our sense of identity. It is, therefore, through an active will that we are able to disidentify from old familiar personality states and awaken enough to recognize from a spiritual point of view the hopeless condition into which we have placed ourselves. This is accomplished through the systematic practice of an exercise Gurdjieff called self-observation. It is a matter of gaining a kind of inner separation so that one "stands aside and watches self go by." Through an active will we are able to create an observing identity which objectively and noncritically is able to separate from the strong habit patterns which have kept us in a "drunken state." It is witnessing consciousness.

This work of self-observation shall, we hope, lead us to a new respect for our physical and emotional bodies. We may find it possible to start transforming many of the ways in which we treat ourselves physically and emotionally and begin to achieve new health at these levels. But the actual goal of self-observation is something even more specific: to remember the real self. Through this exercise of will, we can stand aside and observe the habit patterns of personality. We can finally reach a state in which we remember the real self – that essential identity called individuality. It is at this point that the will leads us to a dramatic shift in consciousness, symbolized in the parable by the driver climbing up to a new level and sitting on the box of the carriage.

But even when moments of this self-remembering are achieved, there remains a problem. The driver does not yet have the reins in hand. The reins symbolize a connection or link between the emotions and thought. Haven't we all frequently experienced the lack of these reins? Our emotions rarely seem to follow in the direction that our thoughts would like, so some connecting discipline is needed. Once again we find, then, an important role for the will to play. A linkage between the horse and driver can be created by the use of purposeful, directed imagination and visualization. The language of the horse is not the same as that of the driver. The mind operates by reasoned thought but the emotions speak a language of imagery. Nicoll puts it this way:

> The horse understands visual language, the driver words, and the parable connects the two. Visual imagery is a universal language. It is the language of signs. The horse only understands a universal language of visual images.

> That is why, if you wish to control the horse from the mind, you must visualize and not merely think. One of the things that we are taught in this Work is visualization. You must visualize what you have thought of in regard to your behavior. . . (*Psychological Commentaries*, p. 467)

The role of the will in helping to create these reins is twofold. On the one hand, we can use the conscious will to purposely direct the mind toward specific visualization. But on the other hand, we might expect a deeper will, what we can call the Real Will, to influence us in a similar way through the imagination. This is a kind of inspired imagination which is so powerful to the soul transformation process. In other words, Real Will can operate on the imaginative forces of the mind to create the very images which can harmonize the activities of thought and emotion.

The parable illustrates another role of the human will in regard to the problem of obtaining guidance. We should take careful note that in this allegory the driver is required to first start the horse and carriage moving, based upon his own best understanding. This shows us something about how to work with inner guidance. We should expect that oftentimes Real Will shall make its intentions evident to us only after we have used the conscious will to set things in motion, only after we have initiated a direction which we tentatively feel is right.

At this point, we come to the conclusion of the parable and its final teaching to us about the will. Once the carriage is set in motion, the driver must be attentive. The hallmark of the will is attentiveness. We can develop a relationship with Real Will only to the extent that we are able to be receptive and responsive. Once again we confront the paradoxical truth: The will is experienced in our lives in an active as well as a receptive mode.

Summary of a New Understanding

We have covered a considerable amount of ground thus far in developing new definitions of the nature of the will as a key ingredient for soul transformation. Perhaps the most important principle is that the will should be appreciated for its extraordinary potential to influence, shape, and direct spiritual growth. But let's keep in mind six other key concepts

1. Will is a *fundamental building block.* We have compared it to one of the primary pigment colors. Along with energy and mind, the will is a fundamental ingredient that determines our experience.

2. The will has both *a conscious and an unconscious component.* It was an extraordinary discovery for humanity when the unconscious nature of the human mind was recognized, and it is an equally significant discovery to find that there is an unconscious level at which the will operates. In fact, a deeper will, more consistent with our real spiritual nature, exists and subtly influences us in waking life if we are attentive to it.

3. The will is our *future.* In this case we are speaking largely of the unconscious component of the will that is sensitive to our spiritual destiny and continually provides us with influences in daily life serving to draw us toward that future. We might even say that this Real Will, coming from our future, can influence the present, particularly through the experience of inspired imagination and feeling.

4. The will stands *in contrast to the mind.* Just as influences from Real Will relate to our future, the mind most often operates from the level of the past. It is the nature of the mind to repeat familiar memory patterns. Even its capability to analyze logically is usually directed toward forms and content which are more related to the past than they are to the future.

Yet, despite this fundamental opposition between mind and will, there is the possibility for cooperation and harmony. Cooperation is possible only if the mind plays an obedient role to the will – only if the mind serves the sense of purpose and direction offered by the will can this cooperative relationship be formed. As long as the mind, with its orientation toward the past, insists upon playing the superior role, the will is left largely in a "sleeping" state.

5. The will is that which gives us our *individuality.* It is not our thoughts that give us our individuality, but instead it is the capacity to

know that we have thoughts. The ability to be self-reflective and stand outside ourselves makes us unique individuals. We experience our specialness in creation because of the capability that the will gives us to be self-reflective. Using the will we can stand aside from or dis-identify from our thoughts enough to recognize that we even have them.

By way of analogy, consider what happens in a lucid dream (a dream in which you know that you are in fact in the dream state). In a lucid dream the will has awakened. In a lucid dream you know of your own individuality as a dreamer, not because you are having thought-form dream images before your awareness, but instead because you are momentarily able to step aside and become self-reflective, recognizing that it is a dream going on about you.

The same principles hold true in waking life. We can learn to go through daily living in a lucid fashion, and it is the will which allows us to have this self-reflective consciousness which knows its own individuality. This is a subtle, and perhaps to some people insignificant, distinction; and yet if we recognize and work with this insight about the significance of the will, it opens up to us a whole array of approaches and techniques for personal transformation. If we can recognize that our very identity as a unique creation rests upon the divine birthright of the free will, then we begin to see its importance and its power in shaping our destiny.

6. We know the will's reality most directly through *attention*. Despite all of these references to an unconscious Real Will, it is crucial for us to work with awakening and training the will as it is experienced at a conscious level. The most immediate way in which we are able to do this is through the capacity to direct attention. The exercise of directing attention can be applied to the outer world of sensory perceptions as well as to our inner world of thought and emotion.

Chapter 6

The Seven Qualities of the Will

If free will is the key to courage, power, and the process of spiritual transformation, it's crucial that we have a clear understanding of exactly *how it expresses in our lives.* We need to broaden our horizons and see that authentic will – as a faculty of our soul life – is something quite different than "will power."

But if will power is not what will is all about, what exactly is it? How exactly do we experience the will, and by what *qualities* can it be recognized?

We can observe certain qualities of the human will, but usually it's in an indirect way. The will usually has a transparent nature and is seemingly invisible. It reveals itself by the physical and mental characteristics which it stimulates.

We observe the same indirect phenomenon with the wind. We don't observe the wind itself but, instead, its effects, as leaves rustle on treetops and discarded papers blow across our path. A similar condition exists with the nature of light. Light itself does not take on physical form and yet it illuminates physical forms so that we can see them. In the same way, the will does not take a physical form and yet we can experience its qualities by the effects it has upon physical conditions. *The will is not an energy and yet we can understand its nature by the way it directs energy. The will is not a state of mind, but we feel its existence by the attitudes and emotions it awakens.*

The analogy of light can be extended further if we recall that white light can be broken down into seven spectral colors. Likewise, the human will has within it seven distinct characteristics. Different life situations provide the opportunity for the will to express itself in various characteristic ways. Here we will explore seven qualities of the will, each of which is in some stage of awakening within you. You may recognize that *some* of these characteristics are ones to which you already have easy access. They are strengths within your character. Others you may recognize as major areas of weakness. Just as pure light is created by the balanced integration of all the colors of the spectrum, each of these qualities of will is necessary for a full awakening of the will's potential within you. Then its transformative power is realized.

These seven qualities were first proposed by Roberto Assagioli, a noted Italian psychiatrist. At his death in 1974 Assagioli left a remarkable legacy of psychological insights and techniques. His system is called "Psychosynthesis," and it is described in great detail in his two principal books, *Psychosynthesis* and *The Act of Will.* Assagioli's system is one of the finest psychologies with a spiritual orientation ever developed. One of the features that makes Psychosynthesis such an extraordinary system is the detail with which Assagioli has documented the role of the will in psychological health. Although only one portion of his book *The Act of Will* deals with the seven qualities of will, it is the section which many readers find most straightforward and immediately applicable. But Assagioli's original contributions about free will can be extended and built upon, as we will do in this chapter.

Each of the qualities of the will can be examined in terms of the way we experience it when the will is healthy. And, in contrast, we can notice what happens in us when that quality is unawakened. In addition, we can recognize that each of these seven qualities of will has a caricature or impostor (such as "stubbornness" posing for "patient persistence"). These bogus qualities resemble the genuine qualities of will; and yet, upon careful scrutiny, they are exposed as lacking the real nature of healthy will.

It's particularly critical to our understanding of the will that we be able to distinguish between the real qualities and their caricature. The will has long been distorted and misrepresented largely because we have been unable to make this distinction. These caricature qualities of will psychologically play a role that can be called the "surrogate will." They operate in the individual's life in a way that so closely resembles the nature of true will that a person may mistakenly assume that the will is healthy. But in those cases, the will is asleep, and a replacement state of mind has usurped its rightful position. [The author wishes to credit his colleague David Aberreg for the insight and naming of "surrogate will."]

The caricature qualities of will have their origin in a fear or a guilt that is often unconscious, yet powerfully influential. They serve *not* to initiate transformation for the individual, but to perpetuate the status quo. No careful study of the seven qualities of will would be complete without an examination of how this illusory, surrogate will imitates certain features of real will, yet lacks its essential ingredients.

Consider then the following seven qualities of the will – all key factors in your capacity to change and transform. Notice which ones seem most healthy in you and which ones are weak or distorted.

1. Vitality: A Dynamic, Energetic Way of Relating to Life

There is an energy fount in the universe, and, as a spiritual creation with free will, you have access to that resource. Yes, there is a physical, mechanistic law of the universe called "entropy," that suggests that the universe is running down. If life is observed as purely physical processes, this law of entropy accurately predicts and describes conditions in the material world. But now from theological and philosophical as well as scientific circles comes speculation that there is a complementary law – a law of syntropy. Conscious, living things of the universe may be special points into which an unlimited energy resource can flow. As a being of free will, you have the capability to create a direct relationship with that limitless supply of energy. This vitality is the first and most fundamental quality of your will.

Your will creates for you an energetic relationship with life by freeing you from energy-sapping patterns of your mind. Those patterns are attitudinal and emotional tendencies which leach your energy, leaving you frustrated and in despair. An act of your will – an act of will drawing upon this first quality – allows you to separate (to "dis-identify") from those energy-sapping mental patterns.

Consider, for example, Rebecca, who is a mother and part-time substitute high school teacher. Rebecca is a worrier. She worries about whether or not her children will do well enough in high school to gain admission to a prestigious university; she worries about her husband's career; and, she worries about her own health, allowing the slightest physical discomfort to stimulate imaginings of impending serious illnesses. Over the years Rebecca has built and rebuilt a complex set of attitudes and emotions, all related to this habitual tendency for worrying. As she gives attention to this pattern of mind, as she allows herself to be so identified with it, it saps and drains her spiritual life force. Her will might make things different, but it's asleep. So, more and more fully, Rebecca's life is governed by the law of entropy. By relating to herself and to life primarily through its physical, material dimension and by allowing this first quality of will to remain dormant, she finds that she is often weak, overwhelmed, and unable to do anything but let her life drift on with its own momentum. Change seems to be out of reach.

What would happen if Rebecca could experience the awakening of this first quality of will? It would allow her to say "no" to these habitual patterns of mind, which have made her the worrier. Her will could give her empowerment in life. She would experience not only a new access to creative life force, but she would also become a dynamic, vital person.

The will is dynamic because it gives you the possibility to make changes in your life. When the will is asleep, your life is static. When the will is unawakened, you merely drift along through life allowing habitual patterns of mind to shape your sense of self-identity and your responses to challenges. However, this first quality of will can move you from a static condition to a dynamic one. The will allows Rebecca to end the hold which these worrying patterns of mind have exerted on her. It allows her to discover that she is empowered to act creatively about each of the areas of life over which she has always worried.

For Rebecca or for you, this first quality of will may manifest as a kind of "quiet enthusiasm" for life. Being full of vitality and having a dynamic, energetic way of relating to life does not necessarily mean a boisterous, extroverted enthusiasm. Because each of us has a different temperament, these qualities of will can manifest in somewhat different ways. The key, however, to this first quality of will is the way in which it gives us a greater access to a universal fount of spiritual energy, allowing and empowering us to make creative changes in life.

We must take great care, however, that we not confuse this genuine quality of will with an imposter: a manic or "hyper" kind of behavior that often looks like vital dynamism but originates in deep psychological imbalances. The manic personality invariably shifts to depression in a short period of time. In its most extreme condition, it reverts to the psychotic state of a manic-depressive individual.

In a related fashion, the "hyper" person is usually someone who is quickly draining herself through busy behavior that looks energetic. This caricature of the first quality of will does not build for her a relationship with the infinite resource of the universe. Instead it draws out and quickly burns up personal energies. It is rarely if ever able to make the kind of genuine life changes which characterize a dynamic, vital existence.

2. Discipline and Control

It should surprise no one that the ability to discipline and control our lives is a feature of the will. In fact, for some people this is the sole quality to which they can easily relate. Unfortunately the stereotyped notions of both self-discipline and self-control fail to do justice to this feature of the will. A broader and healthier view of the role of discipline in personal transformation is needed.

What is also required is an understanding of self-control that truly integrates the human soul, instead of dividing it. Three factors can help you keep this second quality of the will both awake and functioning in a way that aids your growth. First, there is a need for self-control to be linked to vision or a sense of personal ideal. Will operates best in relationship to the present and the future. When you have a vision of how you want your attitudes and behaviors of today to help shape your future, then self-control can more easily stay healthy.

The second key factor is affirmation rather than negation. When you try to use your will's capacity for self-discipline, which of these two options happens most often?

- Things I am going to do
- Things I am *not* going to do

Does your personal voice of the disciplining will say things like "Don't eat desserts" or "Don't be late" or "Don't watch more TV"? Certainly there is a place for using the will to refrain from doing things. However, there is a strong tendency in most all of us to view discipline exclusively in this negative way.

Just as easily, discipline can be *affirming*. You can use your will to "do." For example, the voice of the disciplining will can also say, "Do take time daily to meditate" or "Do spend some time just playing with your kids" or "Do read a new book every two weeks."

Finally, the factor of creativity helps to keep the disciplining, controlling will healthy. Remember that will is the faculty of your soul which stands in opposition to your mind, especially the habits which your mind so potently holds. Sometimes your most disciplined acts can become static, rigid, "positive" habits which have lost all sensitivity to the real needs of the moment. Subtly, something that started out as an expression of real will can turn into unconscious ruts of the mind.

This principle is illustrated at one point in the story of Eric, whose will is in disarray at the level of this second quality: discipline and control. Eric is an energetic, affable 30-year-old carpenter and painter. He is frustrated in his vocational life because it seems like a dead end: he has been unable to reach a supervisory position with any company for which he has worked. Yet the obstacle to his promotion is obvious. He lacks the ability to discipline himself and to gain control over his life. Both at home and on the job, he lacks a sense of direction.

His philosophy of life is that whatever is going to happen will happen. Eric has an admirable aptitude for letting things flow and unfold in their own way, but it is not balanced by any capacity to organize himself in relation to a clear ideal for his future. He has no ability to be co-creative with God because he lacks the skill to control his thinking, feeling, and acting along the pathway of a personal ideal. The second quality of his will is asleep. Sadly, he even fails to exhibit a healthy disciplining will in the one area of his life where he thinks be has achieved it. Four times a week he shows up at a local exercise gymnasium and completes a 45-minute weight-lifting routine. The only interruption to this pattern occurs when he has injured himself in one of the weight-lifting machines. But these mishaps occur with great regularity. Invariably they happen because Eric is determined to force his body to accomplish the 45-minute routine no matter what the extenuating circumstances may be. If he is sick or low on energy one day, he will still "discipline" himself to complete all his regular weight exercises, and often he will strain a muscle in so doing. What started out as a genuine act of a healthy disciplining will has now subtly become something else. He is trapped and enslaved by his own discipline. What began as a promising effort to demonstrate self-control has now become something that controls him.

What is now missing for Eric is a will which is creative in its disciplining, controlling function. Eric needs to awaken a will that is sensitive to the conditions of each day rather than stuck in rigid habits that literally hurt him physically. He also needs a disciplining, controlling will that can help him affirm his talents in order to achieve his potential. When this second quality of his will awakens, Eric can get himself organized to be co-creative in shaping a positive, hopeful future.

However, Eric doesn't need a caricature of this quality of will: repression. Here is the familiar image of "willpower," this imposter quality which usurps the place of a healthy disciplining will. Repression may look like self-control and it may promise growth, but it's really a function of mind acting as surrogate will. Usually motivated by a fear (that may be conscious or unconscious), repression divides the human soul and attempts to "keep the lid on" by denial. Despite its temporary success at achieving self-control, it always fails in the end because that which is repressed doesn't go away.

Instead, a healthy will, manifesting through the quality of self-discipline, says to desires, drives, and appetites, "Your value is appreciated; your energy will be given an appropriate outlet and timing." In sharp contrast, the caricature quality of repression says to those same things within you, "Go away! You are unacceptable in any form and at any time. Let's pretend you don't exist." Psychoanalysts have graphically demonstrated the failure of "willpower" to integrate successfully the personality when it acts through repression. In Jungian terms, the repressed features of yourself merely become a part of your own shadow self.

3. Courageous Initiative

Initiative means the ability to get new things started. Your will is the key to creating new directions for your life. This quality of will initiates novel patterns of living which move you out of the ruts and static habits of your past.

Of course, the creation of new ways of thinking, feeling, and acting involves the mind as well. "Mind is the builder," but it can function in an initiating way only when the will acts to free the mind from its habit patterns. "Will is the director," spurring the mind to the creation of new patterns for living.

The kind of initiative suggested by this third quality of will can relate to both inner and outer changes. Sometimes it means starting different ways of acting in the world. The shy person might begin to speak up more often as an act of will; or, the talkative individual might start to listen more.

However, most fundamentally the initiating will works for an *inner* change. Through it you create a new perspective of yourself and shape a new sense of personal identity. Although the natural tendency is to think of your power to initiate as an outwardly active one, it must be coupled to the more basic inner initiative of new identity.

The word "courageous" is another appropriate description of how you experience this quality of your will. To start something new requires a brave willingness to let go of the old – usually before the new is fully at hand. If you honestly evaluate yourself, you can probably observe the strong tendency to hang on tightly to the familiar ways until the newly created ways are complete. However, personal change usually won't work that way. You must live like a circus trapeze artist who lets go of one swing and dangles in space for a moment before grasping the next swing. Only with courage is that possible. Human growth is achieved only when you have faith in what you are initiating and creating, and thereby courageously let go of the familiar ways of acting or of seeing yourself.

To illustrate this quality, consider the case of Emily, a 62-year-old grandmother and wife of a retired businessman. Emily feels victimized, but not because things are overtly wrong with her life. Her health is reasonably good, she has a family who cares for her, and her material needs are more than adequately met. Yet, because this quality of her will is asleep, she feels boxed in.

All the significant people in her life share a common image of Emily, and she is restless because she feels that she is a victim of their expectations. She never does anything new or unusual since she is so busy conforming to the way everybody assumes she will be. Lacking access to her courageous initiating will, Emily timidly settles for the way things have always been. In relationship to her husband, she gives in to their habitual roles in which he makes all the family financial decisions and she makes all the family social decisions. In relationship to her son, she continues to play a familiar role of nagging and prodding him to take more time for relaxation. In her community, Emily always plays the part of the "second-fiddle" helper in service clubs, doing all the behind-the-scenes work, yet never taking a leadership role.

However, it is within Emily's grasp to change her life, if she can claim the courageous, initiating quality of her will. It might start with an inner activity of her will which bravely surrenders the old way of seeing herself. It can create the vision of a different way of feeling about her talents and how she wants to make use of them. Then, through courageous action she can begin to express this new way of knowing herself. Most likely she won't suddenly and radically alter the way she relates to the world around her. But in little ways she will begin to surprise people. She may speak her mind about an investment her husband plans to make, or ask him to play a bigger role in a family holiday celebration. Or she may startle everyone by offering herself for a leadership role at her church. The feeling of being boxed in and victimized can begin to dissipate, as this quality of her will awakens and gives her the power to be more creative.

What Emily doesn't need, though, is the caricature of this quality of will: reckless novelty. What might try to pose as courageous deeds could actually be actions motivated by hidden fear. This imposter is usually the result of fear-based efforts to bring outer change without making any inner changes at the same time. If Emily suddenly started doing new yet reckless things in her life, it wouldn't be a true act of will, although observers might mistakenly think that she had suddenly become a woman of great courage and strong will. This kind of surrogate willfulness is often recognized by its tendency for destructiveness. In contrast, courageous initiative builds new patterns and directions by adding on new dimensions rather than tearing down old ones.

4. Patient Persistence

The will allows us to live in ways which counter the *appearance* of things. By whatever word you choose to call it, there is a quality within you that can hold to an inner conviction, even when the outer perceptions or the inner memories of the mind suggest otherwise. You may experience it as persistence or commitment or dedication; but, however it happens in your life, it is an indispensable factor in personal transformation.

As already noted many times before, it's the tendency of your mind to repeat the past. It takes persistence and commitment to change, because the mind can present countless reasons for you to abandon your dedication to positive change. But it's your will, which gives you the power to "hang in there" and persistently work toward your ideals.

When this kind of dedication is coupled with real patience, then you have awakened to one of the most dramatic and little-understood qualities of the will. Patient persistence is difficult to grasp for people in our culture because it runs counter to the values and ethics of a technological, consumer society. Men and women of the industrialized Western world have "instantitis," a disease of the mind that expects all problems to be solved immediately. For example, people pop pills to remove pain instantaneously. They watch television dramas which subtly hypnotize them with the belief that most any dilemma can be resolved in one hour.

What is this mysterious factor of patience and how is it related to the will? As we explored in Chapter 3, patience is a way of labeling one of the three fundamental measurements (i.e., dimensions) of our experience in materiality. Patience is an actual dimension of reality - a fundamental ingredient of how you can measure your experiences, just as time and space are dimensions. Patience measures how well you understand the *purposes* for what is happening in time and space. Patience is a way by which you can lift yourself out of the familiar reality which sees life as caught in time. In other words, patience doesn't necessarily mean waiting around for a long time. It doesn't mean suffering gladly for years and years. Patience is outside of time. Admittedly, once you have awakened the dimension of patience, you *might* find yourself choosing to wait for a long time or to suffer gladly for years and years with some problem. But it would be with a patience that brings you understanding.

The relationship between patience and will is intimate. Gurdjieff called patience "the mother of Real Will." As we become more patient, it lifts us to a new perspective of time and space. We see more clearly the purposes behind what is happening to us. We find it easier to be more persistent in working toward our ideals and goals.

When this quality of will is asleep, you may find yourself in a dilemma like the following example: George is a 50-year-old machinist foreman whose life is filled with disappointment. Throughout his adult life his expectations have almost never been met. What he expects of himself, and especially of other people, never measures up. The problem has now become even more serious because George and his family have recently moved to a new city. He has accepted a challenging new job, and he is full of more expectations.

But his disappointment has only been magnified in this new setting. The job hasn't turned out to be what he had hoped. The neighbors surrounding his new home are reasonably friendly, but there is not the strong bond of community he had wanted. George is even disappointed with himself. His new job requires some extra training, and he is disappointed by his frequent failures to grasp many of the new skills he must learn.

What is the heart of George's problem? You might be tempted to say that he is just a hypercritical person. Certainly such a quality can easily lead to this kind of chronic disappointment for anyone. However, in this instance the problem stems from a failure of his will. George lacks the quality of will that would allow him to be patiently persistent in building self-esteem at his new job or in helping build stronger community bonds. When results don't come immediately and easily, George gives up very quickly out of impatience.

Of course, the solution for George doesn't lie with a caricature of will. In fact, there are two imposters that he must try to avoid as he strives to awaken his patiently persistent will. One form of the surrogate will is stubbornness. In this case, he could be persistent but lack the deeper understanding of his problems which comes by patience. People are often fooled by a stubborn individual, and they mistakenly assume that such a person must have a strong, healthy will. In fact, stubbornness is *at best* an activity only of an immature will, a will which is being distorted by fear.

The second caricature of will at this level is a kind of laid-back passivity that is easily mistaken for patience, but which lacks any persistent efforts to make changes. George could just "go with the flow," but that probably won't help his life. Again, people can be fooled by this behavior, assuming that only a healthy will could create such trust in life and be so patient. However, the understanding generated by true patience doesn't lead to passive inactivity. Instead, real patience produces persistent and dedicated commitments to active living.

5. Decisive, Resolute Choice

The most familiar quality of your will is the capacity to choose. It's the most direct way in which you experience your will. Without your will, life would be predetermined and your existence simply mechanical.

But how free is your capacity to choose? Is everything that feels like free will really so free? Behavioristic psychology insists that any feeling of free choice is illusory and that your selections in life are predetermined by your conditioning. The truth of the matter lies between two extremes.

The possibility of a middle ground is appropriate because there are many degrees of freedom. The question of will's freedom is not just between states of "fully on" or "fully off," like a light bulb on a standard switch. Rather there are many points along a continuum of freedom. The extent of your freedom to choose is like a light controlled by a dimmer switch. It can be set to many possible points between full illumination and complete darkness.

Probably much of what feels like free choice is actually very predictable and has a low degree of awakened will. For example, your selections from the menu last time you were in a restaurant may have felt like free-willed choices. But in fact they were probably highly conditioned ones that might have been predicted by anyone who knew your habits and taste preferences. Or, here is another but less obvious example: What about your quick decision to respond sarcastically to the criticism of a friend? It may have felt like a choice, but it really involved conditioned habit with little will.

On the other hand, you do have moments of genuine choice, times when a relatively free expression of your will is possible. Even though these moments may not happen as frequently as you would like to think they do (or as often as it is possible for them to occur), there are opportunities to exercise your decisive, resolute will. If you are a meditator, it happens in those quiet moments as you focus attention. It happens whenever there are two equally attractive courses of action available to you – in your job or your family relations or in the way you treat yourself.

To understand the role that a healthy will plays in making resolute choices, consider this simple model of decision-making. Although decisions you are forced to make often seem messier than this neat three-part scheme, it is still an instructive model to demonstrate how the will can function in either a healthy or a distorted way in confronting choices.

chaos or confusion → recognizing the options → choice

When your will is operating in an awakened and balanced fashion, you pass through all three of these stages for a time period which is appropriate for the problem you face. Obviously there can be no set rules for the ideal amount of time to spend at each step. You don't have much time to move through all three stages when someone yells fire in a crowded restaurant and you smell smoke. On the other hand, if you have just gone through a divorce, it may he wise to spend plenty of time moving through these stages before deciding whether or not to marry again.

When the decisive will is sleeping, you can get stuck at the first or second stage. The result is either a chronic sense of being mixed-up and confused, or it is a pattern of wishy-washy indecision that never gets beyond all the options. First, you need a healthy will just to be able skillfully to recognize the options. In other words, will is a factor not just at the moment of choice, but in a preliminary step that sees all the possibilities. One of the functions of real will is to see shades of meaning, to perceive finer and finer degrees of possibility in a situation. Only then does will play the more obvious role of decision-making. You must have an awakened and balanced will to make effective choices from among the alternatives.

To illustrate this process, consider the case of Carol, a 38-year-old woman who has been divorced for four years. Her life is full of bitterness, not merely toward her ex-husband but also toward the people in her present life situation. She feels unappreciated and robbed of opportunities to be what she could have been. Despite a college degree in business, she has never been able to secure a meaningful position, but has instead bounced around from one part-time job to another. She has been unable to form any close relationship with a man since her divorce, even though she's quite interested in doing so. Her interpersonal relations suffer from the same problem as does her professional life: Carol has a sleeping will, especially in regard to its decisive, choosing quality.

She is a skillful person at recognizing alternatives but gets stuck at that step of the decision-making process. She sees dozens of promising career options in the local business world each year, but is never able to set her sights resolutely on one particular job and commit to it. She has many male acquaintances, a few of whom she knows would like to know her better. However, she is never able to make a choice and then invest the time and energy required to explore the relationship.

A number of psychological interpretations of Carol's condition are obvious. Maybe she fears professional success. Perhaps she is worried, for good reason, about getting hurt again in marriage. But whatever perspective one uses to analyze her situation, the conclusion remains that her bitterness in life can be resolved only by addressing her crisis with her personal will. Nothing can change for the better until she begins to exercise her capacity to make free choices.

As with the other qualities of will, there are caricatures which must be avoided. An imposter will at this level is a tendency to make decisions hurriedly, either skipping one of the steps in the three-part process or just rushing the timing. Each step is important, and effective choices can rarely be made unless the first and second steps are permitted to play their roles.

Confusion and chaos are signs of the old structures of life breaking down so that something new can emerge. There is nothing inherently unspiritual in feeling confused. In fact, growth may not be possible without periods of chaos. Disorientation is a way in which the strong habit patterns of the personality are loosened so that a new pattern of the deeper, more essential individuality can be born. It is a sign of the person with a mature, healthy will that can stand the discomfort of the confusion long enough to let genuinely new, growth-oriented alternatives begin to emerge. To rush the process usually leads only to a limited set of alternatives, ones which will re-create the old state of affairs. For example, if Carol had a caricature of decisive will (rather than merely a sleeping will), she might have tried to rush out of her natural state of confusion after her divorce. Her imposter will might immediately have tried to make the choice of a new marriage partner, with a high likelihood of all alternatives leading to another marriage like her first one.

Another form of the imposter will at this level is to make a choice hurriedly, before all the necessary alternatives have come into view. Of course, the problem one faces is how to know when enough options are present. However, one certainty is that seizing the first option which presents itself is not the mark of a healthy will even though it may fool many observers by its appearance of decisiveness. Healthy will requires at least two alternatives (and sometimes many more, depending on the problem) before it can exercise its quality of decisive, resolute choice.

6. One-Pointed, Focused Concentration

The capacity to concentrate and maintain a singleness of attention is reminiscent of a previous quality of the will: persistence. Whereas persistence is especially related to consistency in action, concentration is most closely tied to the inner mental world. It is an act of will to identify a priority or ideal and then stay focused on it in a one-pointed way.

Although this quality of will is applicable to a wide assortment of life situations, it is especially required in the discipline of meditation, the topic of Chapter 4. There are many schools of meditation and they give different instructions about how to use the one-pointed, focused will. However, almost all forms of this practice recognize the crucial role played by the will. In many meditation systems, the one-pointed, focused will is particularly important to the early stages of meditation. For example, in her classic study of Western contemplatives and mystics entitled *Mysticism*, Evelyn Underhill describes three progressive steps in meditation or "introversion," as she calls it. The three steps are recollection, the quiet, and contemplation.

Especially during the first stage, the will is needed for its capacity to concentrate and focus one-pointedly on the chosen ideal for meditation. This is the most difficult of three stages. It is what Underhill calls "a hard and ungrateful task," and it is well known to anyone who has tried to meditate. The mind does not easily surrender its habitual tendency to flit around from topic to topic, following any stimulus which offers the slightest novelty.

However, the role of one pointed, focused will is not reserved merely for formalized efforts like meditation. Throughout the day you are challenged to awaken and make use of this quality. You are continually faced with opportunities to select priorities for how you may use your time, energy, and other resources. To what extent are you able to maintain a consistent attentiveness to the ideals and direction which you have chosen? Without this sixth quality of will, even the wisest decisions and choices you have made can produce little impact for transformative change.

The key to the will's capacity to be one-pointed and focused is attention. As William James astutely pointed out nearly one hundred years ago, the principal faculty of the will is its capacity to direct attention. When the will is asleep, your life is scattered and distracted. Attention bounces from one thing to the next. With no force to keep it in place or to give it direction, attention rests upon whatever is momentarily most stimulating.

But there is a specific strategy for strengthening this quality of the will. What is required in order to give the one-pointed will a chance to develop and mature? It must have a *focal point*, but not just any focal point. The developing will requires something very special to which it can direct attention. In order to have the best chance to awaken in a healthy, balanced way, it needs a focal point which relates to deep feelings. It involves working with personal ideals and priorities. Of course, it is necessary first to choose ideals, but then of equal importance is the challenge of maintaining focus and concentration on those same ideals as one moves through life.

You have, no doubt, experienced in your own life the realization that deep feelings are a key ingredient for staying attentive and focused. It is much easier to stay focused on something for which you have strong positive feelings, than it is to concentrate on something dry and lifeless. Just think about the qualitative difference between a moving lecture full of stories which evoke strong positive feelings and an abstract presentation that is only intellectual. Which one is more likely to keep you alert? At which lecture are you more likely to find your attention flitting around the room and away from the speaker?

The ideal you choose is the best focal point to help your one-pointed will to develop. An ideal is a deeply felt motivator for living, not an intellectual abstraction that says "ought" or "should." An ideal invites and holds attention because it evokes reinforcing feelings which make attention more likely to remain in place.

However, as straightforward and simple as all of this may sound, most people have very little capacity to concentrate. You can quickly discover this for yourself just by sitting quietly and trying to focus attention for a few minutes in meditation. But the absence of this quality isn't a problem for meditation alone. Because this quality of will is usually asleep, we experience a wide range of difficulties in life.

Consider, for example, Nathan who is a 45-year-old business executive. Although his life has all the appearance of success, he is still troubled. His excellent salary, beautiful home, and handsome family don't erase the fact that he is plagued by a nagging physical ailment. Nathan has a chronic problem with his digestive system that is diagnosed as nervous bowel and which could easily progress to colitis. His physician can find no physical cause for his ailment, and Nathan was told that it is psychologically produced.

He would probably be surprised to learn that his problem is produced by a failure of his will. It is the farthest thing from his mind that his intestinal difficulties are the indirect result of one quality of his will being asleep. Yet, on careful analysis of his life patterns, this is exactly what can be found.

Nathan finds it extraordinarily hard to keep his attention in the present moment and on what is at hand. He is such a good planner and such an anticipator that he is almost never able to be at peace with the present moment. He usually fails to focus his mind one-pointedly on what he is doing. Even when he is getting something done, another part of him is already off in his imagination anticipating the next task.

Such an orientation to life has made him "productive and successful," but it has also produced a sick body. The key to his problem lies with his will. His body is likely to keep giving him these warning signs. It can get well only when he learns to awaken his will enough to be able to give his attention purposefully in a one-pointed and focused way to the present moment. He must learn to stop allowing it to dance around nervously in an imagined future.

However, a healthy capacity to concentrate and focus should not be confused with the caricature of will at this level. There is an imposter of the will called obsession. It may resemble in many ways one-pointedness and concentration, but it is produced by fear or guilt. It is a bogus, surrogate will that does not lead to a healthy personality.

Obsession has the feature of one-pointedness, but it lacks any capacity to help you see reality more clearly. If you are obsessed with making money, your one-pointedness causes you to distort perception. That obsession is probably produced by insecurity – by fear. With this kind of obsession, your view of everything and everybody is twisted into a picture of how you can make your next profit. If you are obsessed with getting love back from a specific person, it produces a tunnel vision. Your view of life is distorted and all other relationships fade in importance.

But obsessions can lead to neurosis, or even worse to serious mental instability. On the other hand, a genuine will serves a different function. It brings you closer to an objective view of the world. Healthy will frees you to see yourself and others with greater clarity and insight.

7. Synthesis and Harmony

Things don't always fit together nicely. But your will allows you to deal with the fragmentary nature of life in a way that is beyond the realm of logic. The will permits you to respond creatively to the contradictions of living and the paradoxes of human nature. So much of what you face in life and in yourself cannot be dealt with satisfactorily using the three-dimensional laws of logic. Without a healthy will, you may find yourself ineffectively trying to achieve wholeness by cutting out or denying parts of life.

For example, what do you do when confronted with contradictions? How do you deal with your own internal paradoxes? Oftentimes the logical mind cannot see any way to synthesize or harmonize differences. Are you serious *and* fun loving? Are you generous *and* tight with money? If things are viewed only from a material perspective, then there seems to be no recourse but to deny or repress one side of the polarity.

What happens if you discover that you are both a person of deep faith *and* a person who doubts and questions? Your logical mind has trouble synthesizing that sort of difference, and it may try to suppress one side or the other. Or, what happens if you find that you are both a person with a great need for others *and* a person who is fiercely independent? How can those equally true and real sides of yourself be integrated? The will is a faculty of your soul which allows you to disengage from the familiar dimension of mind and move to a higher dimension of mind. For example, a three-dimensional, logical mind operates from an assumption of either/or. You can never resolve a paradox or harmonize a polarity from this level of mental functioning.

However, the synthesizing, harmonizing will can move your attention and awareness to a dimension of mind where inclusive resolution is possible (i.e., "A *and* B are both true" rather than "Either A or B is true"). A word to describe the effect of this act of will is *synergy*. Its meaning is described in the adage "the whole is more than the sum of its parts." In other words, there is a way of synthesizing the parts and fragments of life and creating something of a higher order than before (i.e., a higher amount of energy or higher meaning than would be expected, or even a higher dimension of reality).

As a soul, you belong to a higher dimensional reality than what logic can analyze. For you to experience harmony and synthesis of the contradictory aspects of your soul, a quality of will is needed. It can awaken you to the higher dimensional aspects of your mind which operate in an intuitive, holistic, and integrative way. If this kind of will is undeveloped or asleep, the likely result is a life full of disharmony, fragmentation, and confusion,

Consider, for example, the case of Joan who is a 25-year-old graduate student in economics. In addition to her interest in business, finance, and economics, she has been on a long search in her personal life for philosophical and spiritual meaning. Yet she has now arrived at a point of great confusion and cynicism. She has run up against what seem to be insurmountable obstacles created by all the contradictions she has found in life. In the field of economics, she has discovered that all the economic systems and strategies which promise universal prosperity contain flaws which are likely to create new problems as they solve old ones. In her spiritual studies it seems to her that every spiritual truth has a complementary but contradictory additional truth. In her search for self-understanding, she has discovered a perplexing paradox about herself. She is a person who wants to be obedient to a higher sense of order and purpose, but she is also a person who needs her personal freedom.

All of these paradoxes and contradictions have left her confused and cynical about the hopes of ever pulling her life together into a meaningful whole. But her difficulty is not really the creation of a faulty world or imperfect reasoning. Her cynical outlook is the result of a failure of will. Only by awakening her will can she disengage from the influences of her present mental condition. Only by awakening her will can she see both the world and herself from a higher dimensional perspective.

To awaken and develop her synthesizing, harmonizing will, Joan must guard against a caricature of this quality: a kind of synthesizing or blending which doesn't produce the "something extra" of synergy. Instead it reduces everything to norms and averages. The imposter, surrogate will (often produced by laziness) attempts to integrate by blurring uniqueness, by homogenizing life. It loses the individuality of each component as it combines. But true synergy *is* possible because the specialness and distinctiveness of each ingredient part is respected.

Let's look more closely at the difference between these two types of blending. The first type corresponds to impostor will. Imagine that you had three similar bottles of sugar-solution water. The bottles contain solutions of 10%, 20%, and 30% sugar, respectively. If you blend the three in equal quantities, the resultant solution will be an "average" 20% solution. The uniqueness of the three individual components is lost. That is a homogenizing blend that fails to create something bigger.

In contrast, imagine that you play three notes on the piano: C, E, and G. Each note is the sound of a particular rate of vibration, but what is the sound of the three played together as a chord? The chord is *not* a single tonal sound which averages the three components. It is synergistically "something extra" that is created, while the integrity of the three individual notes still exists simultaneously. That is exactly what is possible when a healthy will synthesizes and integrates diversities in life. The mind is lifted by the will to a higher mode of operation from which a whole new view of life is possible. The different notes of life can be experienced as a harmonious chord.

In our example, through a healthy will Joan can escape from her cynicism. As she sees herself and her life from a broader mental outlook, contradictions start to appear as something else. Each pair of polar opposites is a reminder of the richness of life. Each side has its own time and place of rightness, but no single description or theory can capture the whole truth.

A Personal Inventory

Take time to make these seven qualities of your will more personally meaningful. Think about how you relate to them by considering several questions listed below. These questions are meant to serve as an outline for your inventory and personal assessment. But use the questions merely as a starting point. Feel free to let your self-analysis go deeper.

Most likely you will find that some of the seven qualities of your will are more fully awake, operative, and healthy than others of the qualities. You may also find that for some of these qualities, the habit patterns of your mind have usurped the mind's role and now act as an imposter – what we called earlier in this chapter "surrogate will."

There may be major differences among the various areas of your life. For example, you may have a healthy self-disciplining will in only one area of your life – say, daily meditation – but in no other area. You may find that the imposter quality of stubbornness comes up in two principal areas – say, for example, in your relationship with your daughter and your attitudes toward money.

For each of the seven qualities, think about these questions concerning your will:

- In what areas of your life do you sometimes *successfully* express this particular quality?
- In what areas of your life is this quality almost always *asleep*?
- Where in your life do you see signs of this quality's *imposter*?

The Chakras as Centers of Will

Many esoteric traditions describe seven spiritual centers or chakras within each of us. (In the ancient Sanskrit language, this means "wheel" because of the wheel-like vortices of energy which clairvoyants claim they can see at each center.) These traditions teach that the chakras are located within the physical, etheric, and astral bodies. They constitute one of the central models of many spiritual and metaphysical systems. There is general agreement about the approximate location of these seven centers in the body and about the qualities of human consciousness and experience to which they relate. These centers are also sometimes called "psychic centers" because of the way in which they may relate to the awakening of paranormal perception.

Each center acts like a transducer, transmitting influences from more subtle and spiritual dimensions into the denser, more concrete realm of material life. A transducer is generally understood as a device that takes energy from one system in one form and transmits it to another system in a different form. For example, a telephone serves as a transducer by taking electrical impulses from telephone lines and transmitting them to the human ear in the form of sound.

Not only are the spiritual centers described as go-betweens for the spiritual life force moving into the human body, but they are also seen as storehouses of habit. That is to say, each chakra is predisposed by conditioning or learned memories to operate in particular ways. For example, the fourth spiritual center relates to the consciousness of human love. Suppose you have mentally built patterns of jealousy and envy with your attitudes and emotions. In this case, your efforts at human love have been distorted and become selfish. But where does that habit pattern live? The predisposition may be encoded in the physical brain, but the tendency is stored in the subtle energy patterns of the fourth chakra, as well.

The following chart describes the location of each center and the positive qualities of consciousness associated with it.

7	top of the head	oneness; spiritual healing; universal love
6	behind the forehead	higher mind integrating intellect and intuition; the third eye of spiritual vision
5	throat	choice; decision
4	heart	human love and sympathy
3	solar plexus	the use of force or power in earthly expression
2	lower abdomen	the polarity of yin/yang or feminine/masculine
1	groin or base of spine	survival and nurturance of physical self; survival of the species through reproduction

This chart is merely the sketchiest of outlines. However, with this basic chart in mind, it is possible to proceed with a look at how the seven qualities of will just described are related to the seven centers. Some systems of thought have suggested that *only* the fifth center is related to the will – that, it is *the* will center. However, if we keep in mind these two points, it would seem to make more sense that *all* the chakras are "will centers."

(1) The nature of the will is far broader than just choice and decision-making.

(2) The chakras are consciousness centers, and consciousness is the product of mind and will in interaction.

The following column might, therefore, be added to the chakra chart above. The seven qualities you have explored in this chapter were presented in a numerical order to correspond to the seven centers:

7 Synthesis and harmony, which helps you attain oneness

6 Focused, one-pointedness, which characterizes the higher mind

5 Decisiveness, which allows you to choose

4 Patient persistence, which is required in human loving

3 Courageous initiative, which expresses your power to effect change in material life

2 Discipline and control, which allows the poles of yin and yang to be balanced

1 Vitality and dynamic living, which allows you to have the resources to survive

Anyone who is working with the chakras model as a tool for meditation or personal transformation can see the value of this additional column. It suggests the very qualities which must be awakened in order to transform.

Assagioli's model of seven qualities of the will is an extraordinarily useful one. It brings the will from an abstract, metaphysical concept into the immediacy of daily living. It allows each of us to see where relative strengths and weaknesses lie. Nevertheless, it does not offer a complete story of how to awaken and develop the will. In the next chapter we'll explore another model about the human will and personal transformation – this one, a theory of how will develops through stages.

Chapter 7

Stages in Developing Your Will

How can you develop your will? Once you feel a willingness to change, what can you do to make your will healthier so that real transformation of your life becomes possible. Having seen some of the will's characteristics and qualities in the last two chapters, you may still need a strategy for awakening the capabilities which it promises.

In this chapter and the next you'll have the chance to explore will development in its many facets. Chapter 8 presents a set of specific training exercises. But first, let's consider here in Chapter 7 a more fundamental set of ideas.

Your will goes through distinct stages of evolution as it awakens within you. The concept of developmental stages is familiar to many fields of study. For example, mathematics has a time-tested curriculum in which the student is led through a series of developmental steps in knowledge. First, the student learns to count and then to add and subtract. Only after these fundamentals are mastered can the student move on to multiplication, division, and fractions. Later, mathematical subjects such as algebra can be added, as well as the more advanced topics like calculus. Each new stage builds upon the previous one.

But does the same kind of neat, systematic sequence apply to the building blocks of the human soul – spirit, mind, and will? If the spirit is thought of as the fundamental energy of the universe, then the scientific model of vibratory rates demonstrates distinct stages. Ranging from extremely low frequency radio waves to the highest frequency x-rays, at least one kind of orderly, sequential expression of energy exists. That scientific model of energy doesn't tell the whole story of spirit, but it nevertheless suggest a valuable model.

Perhaps even more suggestive of developmental stages is the way the human mind can be experienced. Many psychological theories refer to layers of mental activity, and only one of those layers is the familiar mental state of conscious thinking and perceiving. As awareness moves to mental regions which are usually unconscious, then more expansive states of mind are available. It may be like peeling layers of an onion; and as awareness moves deeper and deeper into the psyche, then higher dimensional expressions of mind are possible.

In fact, a simple way of describing a developmental, growth sequence for mind expansion is: first, the conscious mind; then, the subconscious mind; and finally, the superconscious mind, Of course, there may be substages, as well as traps where the developmental unfolding can get stymied.

Anyone who has tried to meditate knows how true this is. As you begin to quiet the normal, conscious mind and seek contact with the superconscious mind, what happens? You begin to contact material from your subconscious mind. At first, it may be recent thoughts and memories that have not been tucked away for long. As you become more quiet and focused in meditation, deeper elements of your subconscious may pop into your awareness. How easy it is to be distracted by all of this! How readily the true goal of meditation periods can get lost if you become caught up in these mental digressions.

However, remember that there are not three different minds, but instead three distinct ways that the oneness of mind can be experienced. We must not be misled at this point, as we think about any kind of developmental stages. For example, there is a oneness to the law of mathematics, and multiplication tables and algebraic laws are two different ways of experiencing mathematics. In a similar fashion, a five-stage sequence of will development (soon to be described) does not refer to five different wills. Instead, there is a oneness of will within your soul, but there are growth steps in how you can experience it.

The classic three-stage model of mind development (as described above) has at least one important difference from the example of a mathematical curriculum. In learning mathematics, the student cannot expect to have any (even momentary) experiences out of the prescribed curriculum order. While learning multiplication the student cannot expect to have temporary "leaps ahead" momentarily to grasp calculus theory. However, such leaps ahead can and do happen within the developmental stages of the mind (as well as with the stages of will development to be described shortly). For example, a visionary experience may give you a temporary glimpse of the superconscious mind. Or, a spontaneous psychic experience may give you a momentary taste of certain aspects of the subconscious mind. The stages are, therefore, not rigid but contain a certain measure of flexibility. *You can expect to experience advanced stages of mind or will, but should not count on being able to maintain them until the previous stages are mastered.*

What, then, would a developmental sequence for will look like? In the curriculum of will growth, what corresponds to learning mathematical addition, or algebra, or calculus? Since the metaphor of "awakening the will" has frequently been used, perhaps a good starting point would be to examine how the very process of awakening in the morning has stages which build upon each other. Imagine that you are in bed asleep, a stage where no degree of awakening has yet taken place. Suppose that on this particular morning you won't he jarred awake by an alarm clock, but instead you can gradually awaken at your familiar time. The first stage of awakening is the hypnopompic state in which the inner world of your dreams is mixed with hazy, diffuse perception of the physical environment in your bedroom. In this half-sleep state you are not clear about where you are. This stage may last for seconds or many minutes.

Following this, a distinctly different stage emerges in which you become a little more awakened. At this next stage, you are "back in your body" – you come back to your sense of personality and may lazily entertain disjointed, vague thoughts about last night's dreams or what's coming up in the day ahead. But in this stage of wakefulness you probably still find it hard to get out of bed.

Next, your wakefulness can increase to a stage where you feel the desire to be up and get started on the day. This stage of wakefulness is sufficient for such early morning tasks as washing your face or putting bread in the toaster. However, you probably aren't sufficiently awake at this stage to do things like balance your checkbook or other challenges which require sustained and alert attention. Only later in the morning routine do you realize you've fully awakened and that you are ready to tackle most any task. In this last stage you are as fully awake as you will become during the course of a day.

These steps are presented not as the stages of will development, but rather as an *analogy* of how an awakening process progresses through levels and degrees. The will has its own distinctive characteristics for each stage of development; and, like getting up in the morning, each stage builds upon mastery of previous stages.

In psychological and spiritual literature dealing with the will, little attention has been given to any sort of progressive development through stages. Assagioli discusses "aspects" of the will (as a topic separate from his seven "qualities") but makes no attempt to link the aspects into a systematic growth sequence. Other systems have proposed a conscious and an unconscious will, but without a clear description of progressive steps in awakening and harmonizing the two.

But a new understanding of will development is possible. The remainder of this chapter describes a multistage model. This is likely to be a somewhat complex theory, which requires careful reading and serious thought about human psychology. *The key to authentically transformative change is to engage all these development stages of the will.*

This model of the stages of will has five steps which are sequentially numbered from 0 to 4. The number 0 is chosen for a starting point because it accurately describes the amount of will present at its starting point for growth. As you read the description for each stage, you are likely to recognize that parts of your daily living seem to fit particular stages. In other words, you are probably *not at any single stage* in the development of your will. Instead you may find that one stage of will development clearly defines how you interact in certain relationships and situations, whereas a different stage better describes how you use your will in response to other circumstances. Unfortunately, most of us have very few parts of life where stages 1 though 4 are applied frequently. The most common human responses of life come from stage 0 of will development, so that level invites our immediate attention.

Stage 0: The Sleeping Will

Your will typically exists in a sleeping or unconscious state. You and all those you encounter are, for the most part, walking around through life "asleep." In other words, that which is most essentially real and true about you as a spiritual being is in an unconscious state, largely because of the unawakened state of your will.

The principle is most clearly described by distinguishing between two levels of your being: your *personality* and your *individuality*. These terms were introduced in Chapter 2. Your personality is the acquired set of habit patterns with which you most often operate in life. Your personality traits have largely been learned from parents, teachers, television, etc. They are made up of countless mechanical ways in which you think, feel, and act in the world. In others words, your personality is your familiar sense of identity, but it exists by habit and routine. It's your conditioning.

Your personality is reactive. In an automatic and very predictable way, it responds to the events of physical life. For example, if someone says something distasteful to you, your personality responds like a machine with automatic thoughts, feelings, and behaviors. No real will is involved, any more than your automobile "wills" to start its engine when you turn the ignition key. Some of the responses of your personality are "nice" and some "not so nice." However, what *all* these automatic reactions have in common is their lack of conscious, willed selection. You are "asleep" in your personality – that is "asleep" to your real identity.

But as individuality, you are a being of will. When you are aware of and identify with individuality, you are able to make choices and be creative. Of course, your individuality is not a perfect self, because it needs to grow and evolve itself. From the level of individuality you are an unfolding spiritual being. This is the identity that is capable of growth, whereas your personality exists to repeat patterns and largely stay the same.

Often it isn't easy to distinguish influences of your individuality from those of your personality. Part of the problem comes from the fact that the personality contains many subpersonalities. Each one is a role that you occasionally play in life, a particular sense of "I" with which you identify. Because every subpersonality conforms to the characteristics of personality in general, each separate "I" is relatively devoid of will. On the one hand you may notice that your various subpersonalities seem to have separate and conflicting "wills," but on close examination what looks like will is actually the surrogate will of ingrained habit trying to repeat itself.

Each subpersonality has its own set of habitual ways of thinking, feeling, and acting. Each one also thinks of itself as the "whole show" whenever it is "on stage" (i.e., each has the momentary attention of consciousness). Each subpersonality may try to be sincere; but because of the constantly shifting sense of which "I" you are, it is difficult for you to be consistent in life.

For example, suppose that, at 6:00 p.m., you are reading a book about meditation which deeply inspires you. At that moment, the subpersonality that has your attention, the "I" you think yourself to be, is one which could be labeled "the enthusiastic seeker." In that role you say to yourself, "I'm going to get really serious about meditation and even start getting up at 3:00 a.m. to have a daily meditation period." That aspect of your personality really means it. But in the moment of making such a vow, that subpersonality has forgotten that it is not the whole story of who you are. So, 3:00 a.m. comes, the alarm goes off, but not it is not "the enthusiastic seeker" that rolls over in bed to turn off the alarm. It is a personal sense of identity that might be "the exhausted parent." The planned meditation period doesn't happen.

Whether or not you can personally relate to *this* particular example is not important. No doubt you can think of several examples that *are* relevant from your own life. They are instances in which a shifting sense of personal identity results in intentions not being followed.

Stage 1: Negating Will

Stage 1 is a first step toward disengaging from the control of the personality self and allowing the influence of the individuality self to come into play. Recall the analogy of the personality wheel that was presented in Chapter 2 (perhaps even going back and restudying that section). There is an automatic-pilot quality to the way in which the personality self turns like a wheel. And that leads to a question you face in the development of your will: If I am identified with my personality wheel in some part of my life, how can I change, how can I awaken my will enough to resist the mechanical, habitual reactions that are so familiar?

Ironically, the movement from Stage 0 to Stage 1 is often motivated by one of the self-centered drives of the personality. Often it is ambition or pride. Or, sometimes it is the desire to escape the emotional or physical pain that is continually being re-created by the personality. But whatever the impulse, the first small awakenings are the beginning of a more objective consciousness of life. These initial stirrings of will create the opportunity to shape one's own sense of identity and begin the shift from knowing self as personality to knowing self as individuality.

Of course, these first awakenings of will are not very mature expressions. They may be like a child trying to grow up, whose first efforts at adult approaches to life may look awkward. The first stage of will development is merely the capacity to say "no," to set limits by negating, even to use so-called willpower to repress what is undesirable. We also saw in Chapter 2 just how important it is to be able to set boundaries in one's life.

How awakened is your own will at this stage in your life? If you are at Stage 0 of development, with little or no will awakened, then from this highly subjective state you have surrendered all control to your mind and its conditioning. Your actions in life are really reactions based on habit. Your sense of personal identity in any moment is determined fully by material life conditions and what they stir up in you. But if your will is active, there may be some genuine choice in your action and in your sense of who you are.

It all begins with Stage 1: the initial awakenings of will. Here we find the beginnings of self-reflection. At Stage 1, you start to feel that your personal identity is not necessarily equivalent to what your mind is presenting at the current moment. You begin to distinguish your self-identity (i.e., "Who am I?") from the emotions and attitudes that flood automatically into your awareness. As elementary as this may sound, most of us spend very little of the day with the will awakened to even this first stage. Instead, we tend to remain "asleep," allowing the habitual mind to totally shape who we feel ourselves to be. If you doubt this, observe yourself carefully for a day, even for an hour. You may notice how often your sense of "I" changes without your having chosen to do so. You may notice how automatic most of your actions are.

This first degree of awakening is not easy. It is a tenuous hold that we first have upon this birthright called the will. Because the movement out of sleep is so difficult, the early awakenings of will are rather crude and even negative in character. But isn't this true of most beginnings? Our early efforts to walk were awkward and poorly controlled; our initial attempts to feed ourselves were messy. In a similar way, the first stage of will development is a sort of negative will: the capacity to say "no." For this reason we might label this stage of will "negating will."

Will, at the first stage, attempts to forge a new sense of personal identity by rejecting the impressions presented by the mind. It takes on a variety of appearances: rebellion, negation, even the Victorian "willpower" or the capacity to reject temptations.

To put another label on this stage of development, we might call it "adolescent will" – not because it is uniquely characteristic of teenagers, but because the images of the young person trying to form his or her new sense of identity apart from parents and family illustrates well the process. Imagine a 15-year-old boy who is getting dressed up to go out on a date. He puts on his brown suit and loud, paisley tie, only to have his mother come in and loudly demand that he change to his brown tie. We all know what typically follows. Even if the boy inwardly recognizes that his mother is "right," it is more important to him that the newly emerging integrity of his own personhood be respected. Using Stage 1 will, he rebels; he shouts "no" to her demands. Here the will has been used to distinguish his own needs and identity from what his mind presents to him: the sights and sounds of his mother, and the memories of his past childhood where she was the authority.

With Stage 1 will, there is a quality of repression inherent in negating the influences from the mind. If Stage 1 is followed by further will development, this sort of temporary repression can be healthy because it allows the experience of a clear feeling of unique personhood. However, if you never go any further than "willpower," such repression is likely to be detrimental. Stage 1 is a positive step in the use of the will to the extent that it allows you to dis-identify from patterns of mind that have been controlling your sense of personal identity and your responses to life. This kind of negating allows you to stand apart from old patterns of mind and create a new sense of yourself.

We all have personally meaningful expressions of how first-stage will manifests in our lives. For one person, it is that which says, "I am not going to eat another piece of that pie which my mind is telling me would taste very good." For another person, it is that which says, "I am not going to give in to that old feeling of resentment which my mind is telling me is the justifiable way to react to this individual." An effective self-observation exercise for each of us is to watch for the ways in which these stirrings of will awaken and manifest in our lives.

Stage 2: Skillful Will

The will awakened to its second stage is more than just an intensification of qualities from the first stage. The second stage is characterized by the ability to *blend and synthesize.* At Stage 1, the integrity of one's individuality was created by rejecting influences coming from the outside world or even voices within one's own mind. But now, at Stage 2, the sense of individuality has grown stronger, and it's possible to use will to reconnect with what had to be rejected before.

The second stage might be labeled "adult will," again not so much because all adults demonstrate this development, but because our idealized notion of what it means to be adult-like includes characteristics bestowed by this level of the will. The adult is expected to be able to create skillfully a blend of two factors:

- An inner knowledge of what one's own unique individuality wants and needs in the present moment.
- The vast array of influences coming from other people, the environment, and one's own attitudinal and emotional past.

At Stage 1 of the will, differences between these two factors were resolved by the second factor being rejected in favor of the first. But now a new means of resolution is possible. "Adult will" skillfully blends the genuine needs coming from one's own individuality with the demands and expectations arising from the outside world or the demands from memories in our own minds.

What does Stage 2 will feel like? Take the example of being tempted to eat another piece of pie. Stage 1 negating will would use willpower, repressively saying "no" to the memory of how good pie tastes and the desire immediately to repeat the experience. However, Stage 2 skillful will might express itself as, "I know that pie would taste good and I am going to have some more – but not right now. I'll pick a more appropriate time."

Or, consider the case of the 15-year-old who is told by his mother to switch to the brown tie. We might expect that, when a similar event occurs ten years after this time, the now 25-year-old adult would respond differently to his mother. His own sense of unique personhood is less vulnerable, and he can more skillfully blend inner and outer demands than he could when he was 15. If the dressing up with a paisley tie episode were to reoccur, he might be able to respond out of Stage 2 will saying, "Mother, you are right, that brown tie would look good with this suit. Next time I wear this suit, I think I will wear it. But tonight I am going to go ahead with what I think looks just as good."

Admittedly, these examples are a bit simplistic. Often life offers challenges with much more complex issues in which pat answers don't work. But the principle remains the same in any situation we confront. There is a level of the will from which we can operate that does not require us to be stubborn or negative in affirming our sense of individuality. No doubt, there are times when Stage 1 will is the more appropriate stage from which to operate, but often the appropriateness is because of our own needs for development and growth – and not so much something inherent in the event.

From time to time in our lives, we all need to cycle back to Stage 1. It is not a developmental step that is reserved for teenagers. In fact, if you carefully observe yourself, you shall likely see that in a typical day your will awakens and falls back to sleep many times. You probably see that you spend most of the day at Stage 0, some time at Stage 1 and only brief peak moments at Stage 2.

Another label for Stage 2 will is the "redeeming, nurturant will." With your sense of unique personhood and individuality established by Stage 1 will, it is possible to go back and re-embrace those patterns of mind which you negated and repressed at Stage 1. In this fashion there is an archetypically feminine quality to Stage 2 will, in contrast to the active (even harsh) character of the more masculine Stage 1 will.

The "redeeming, nurturant will" is able to direct attention so as to find, within the patterns of mind previously rejected, *something* which is judged good. For example, the 25-year-old young man can now use Stage 2 will to re-embrace his mother's criticism. He can recognize some *aspect* of her criticism with which he can agree. Stage 1 will has made him strong in his sense of individuality, and now he need not fear being overwhelmed by memories of his childhood and mother's authority. He is able to use Stage 2 will to find the essence of caring within his mother's behavior and respond to it rather than to the strident form her criticism takes.

What helps to keep your will healthy at Stage 2? An acceptance of the contradictory, paradoxical nature of life. Because spiritual reality is of a higher dimension than physical life, higher truth often manifests as paradoxical opposites. For example, since you are a being of greater dimension than the three-dimensional physical world, you have within you many contradictory sides – all of which have their own measure of validity. The same fact holds true of any person you encounter. Although your logical mind has trouble with paradoxes and would prefer to have truth just one way or the other, an understanding of the paradoxical nature of life can help you see the role that can be played by a healthy, skillful will. It may be easier to use the will at Stage 1 to repress certain sides of yourself. It may be easier to use negating will to say "no" to certain aspects of other people. It shows a real development of will to use it skillfully and find ways to balance and unify the many sides of life.

Stage 3: Empowering Will

A dramatic change takes place with the third level of development. Up until now, the relationship between mind and will has had a consistent character. The mind has been the "senior partner" in the pair. Now the will awakens sufficiently so that the balance begins to shift.

We can label this stage of development "empowering will" – something quite different from "willpower." With the will awakened to this third step, you recognize that no influence of mind is stronger than the will. The feeling which is created says, "I am quite independent of anything my mind may present to me for experiencing." With this recognition comes a tremendous sense of control and power over life.

This stage of development is beautifully demonstrated by lucid dreaming. Recall that this curious phenomenon consists of the awareness that you are in a dream *while the dream is still going on.* It is a fairly rare occurrence for most dreamers, but one that is not easily forgotten because of its novelty and great impact. The term "lucid dream" has frequently been misunderstood to imply any dream that is especially clear; for example, one in which the symbols are straightforward and transparent; or, for a dream in which the interpretation is literally given while one is still in the dream. However significant those kinds of dream examples may be, they do not describe lucid dreams. Rather the term is used strictly for a special event that occasionally happens in our dreams: the recognition of dreaming while the dream is still going on.

What do such lucid dreams have to do with the will? In a typical (i.e., non-lucid) dream, you are in a highly subjective state, with little or no will present. Even the dream experiences in which you seem to be making choices are probably more a matter of unconscious habit patterns, with mind doing the choosing. There is virtually no self-reflection or recognition of your sense of individuality. But something very different takes place in a lucid dream: The will awakens.

With the introduction of lucidity, you recognize that you have identity and individuality apart from the dream events. In saying, "This is merely a dream state," what are you the dreamer actually asserting? You recognize that this dream world is somehow distinct from the normal world of physical life. For example, consider this actual lucid dream:

> I'm in a dark, poor section of a city. A young man starts chasing me down an alley. In the dream, I'm running for what seems to be a long time. Then I become aware that I am dreaming and that much of my dream life is spent running from male pursuers. I say to myself, "I'm tired of this never-ending chase." I stop running, turn around and walk up to the man. I touch him and say, "Is there anything I can do to help

> you?" He becomes very gentle and open to me and replies, "Yes. My friend and I need help." I go to the apartment they share and talk with them both about their problems, feeling compassionate love for them both. (*Lucid Dreaming* by Scott Sparrow, A.R.E. Press, 1978)

In this dream, self-reflection awakens sufficiently so that the dreamer (a woman) recognizes an identity apart from the image which her mind is presenting in the dream. In a typical dreaming state, she would have responded subjectively to the events of the dream. She probably would have run or fought. The outer dream events would have shaped her identity as a pursued, fearful person. But with lucidity, the will acts potently to create a sense of identity which differs from the influences from the dream. From this new feeling of identity, she responds in a creative, loving fashion; and, in return, the images of mind (i.e., the dream symbols of the men) alter their behavior and attitude.

This dream beautifully illustrates an effective use of will at the first and second stages, and then it concludes with will at the third stage: "empowering will." With the awareness and words, "I'm tired of this never-ending chase," the dreamer demonstrates the skillful, redeeming, nurturant will of Stage 2. Then, at the third level, mind becomes the servant of will, as demonstrated in the dream when the images and events change.

Oftentimes, however, empowering will is not used in such a constructive manner. In fact, this third stage of development is a critical, even dangerous, point. The possibility and temptation arise to use the will to serve selfish or limited ends. In a lucid dream, the tendency is to use the newfound power of awakened will to manipulate the dream content. Such experiences are quite possible and available with this level of will. Most people who have had lucid dreams have discovered such remarkable capabilities. They find that they can escape from uncomfortable dream images by just flying away, or by wishing or willing the undesirable images of mind to change into something else.

In the example quoted above, the woman might have used her lucidity in a less constructive way. She could have turned to her pursuers and used her will to imagine them as friends or benevolent beings. No doubt, such dream manipulation could have taken place. But in doing so she would have avoided something within her in need of healing – it would have been disrespect for the integrity of the dream. Admittedly, the dream images did change once her lucidity emerged. However, it was *not* because she tried to overwhelm the dream images with the power of her will. Instead, she used the power of her will to create a constructive, fear-free sense of her own identity, and then the dream began to change as a natural result.

What, we might ask, does all this have to do with making transformative changes in daily living? The answer is that the process experienced in a lucid dream is very similar to what is possible in physical conscious life. We can learn "lucid living." It may not be experienced in daily life exactly in the way it is in the dream state. However, both involve awakening the will to this stage we call "empowering will."

When the empowering will emerges, a fundamental shift in perception takes place. In the dream state, the perceptual shift creates the view that "this is only a dream" and, therefore, a feeling of invulnerability. In physical life, the perceptual shift creates the view that the world presented by the physical, conscious mind is actually the past and not the present.

This recognition is a radical change in how we view life. At this third stage, not only has the balance of influence shifted from the mind to the will, but now the mind is experienced as primarily an agent of the past. A careful analysis shows that this, in fact, makes sense, even though it is contrary to the way in which we are accustomed to seeing things. Recall what we already explored in Chapter 3 about time and transformation. In fact, transformative change requires a shift in consciousness about our place in the scheme of time.

Your attitudes and emotions are patterns of mind which merely reflect your past experiences. When you feel angry or jealous, the emotional experience is largely determined by past events. The anger you may feel today is real; but its energy has been patterned and formed by circumstances in your past.

But not only are the internal attitudes and emotions recognized as being of the past, we recognize that the external, physical world is the past also. On the one hand, this notion sounds nonsensical. But consider the implications of the universal law, "The spirit is the life, mind is the builder, and the physical is the result." That law simply states that everything which we experience as physical reality (e.g., our bodies, material objects, etc.) has been created first at the dimension where mind is the builder. Initially mind creates, and then later (perhaps seconds later or perhaps years later) the pattern of energy manifests in physical form. The findings of psychosomatic medicine illustrate this law very well as it relates to our physical bodies. Through your state of mind you build the relative health or disease of your body. Your body is a concrete, material expression of your past. The law works in a similar fashion for other objects or events we experience as physical reality.

The awakening of your will at the third state – empowering will – brings this recognition: Your mind no longer has such a hold on you because you realize that the impressions brought to you by your mind are images and influences of the past. They *are real,* but your tendency up until now has been to misinterpret them and to give them an unwarranted control in shaping your own sense of who you are. Even with this level of awakening, the mind still functions as the builder, but it is as the servant-builder under the direction of the will. At this third stage your will is an initiator, directing the building of new patterns by your mind.

But if mind is that which gives you impressions of the past, then what is the *present*? Your inner response. Your sense of who you are in the situation. For example, suppose you are at a dinner party and someone makes an insulting remark to you across the table. If you are metaphorically asleep, at Stage 0 of the will, then you react in a subjective way. Your inner sense of who you are is determined by whatever emotional pattern arises from your subconscious mind in response to what you have just heard. You may toss a similar insult back.

But if you have awakened your will to Stage 1, you resist the inner emotional pattern and have the "willpower" to keep silent. At Stage 2 you find something to say or do which skillfully blends an appreciation for the other person's dislike for you along with the clear awareness that your real identity is not what the insulting remark implied. Perhaps this would be a good-humored comment which takes note of the feeling behind the other person's attack but, at the same time, proposes a different picture of who you are. It skillfully invites your antagonist to see you in a new way.

However, with the third stage of will development another option in this story is introduced. With empowering will, you recognize that the feelings and comments of the other person are actually images of his or her past. What you are seeing and hearing is not really the present of that soul, but rather a physical expression of experiences from the past. You also recognize that your own emotional reactions of outrage and resentment are patterns of energy arising from your own past. All of this is quite real, and yet the will allows your awareness to be in the actual present moment. The will allows you to choose your identity – to be your real individuality. Then, whatever response you do make can be creative and can represent the best in you.

To depict this in a diagram, notice that the mind tends to draw you back to the past. Even its building and creating function has the *tendency* to re-create and reinforce patterns from the past. When the will is awakened, it draws you into the future. *When your will is in charge and creatively directing your mind, transformative change happens and movement toward your destiny is possible.*

PAST	← NOW →	FUTURE
Influence of mind without awakened will		Influences from the awakened will

In the example above, Stage 3 will is described in a healthy mode. However, it doesn't always work that way. As one is empowered by will, that power is not always used constructively. The third stage of will development is a potentially dangerous one. Particularly at this level the will can be used to fulfill selfish aims rather than altruistic ones. With the sense of personal power it provides, you can literally lead yourself astray. Without a spiritual purpose to keep yourself directed, the influence of the will over the mind can get you even more deeply entrapped in a mistaken identity for yourself.

For example, consider again the moment you become lucid in a dream. How is your will used in this opportune situation? As already mentioned, some lucid dreams practice a form of dream manipulation. The will is used to wish things which have been desired but unfulfilled in daily life (e.g., having a dream imagery affair with a sexually desirable person who is unobtainable in waking life). However, this may not be a wise decision. Such dream manipulation using empowering will creates patterns of mind which do not dissolve upon awakening from the dream. Such inner behavior is as unsound for personal ecology as is tossing trash from one's car window, thinking to be rid of it. There is a more appropriate way to deal with unwanted trash, just as there are better ways to deal with desires and fantasy needs.

Stage 3 is the danger zone of will development because one can misunderstand this level, believing it to be the final step, the goal. If you don't feel something still ahead – the transcendent – there is the temptation to use the power of this level to strengthen the desire patterns of your personality. Furthermore, a person who has awakened will to this level can have a remarkable influence over those other people who have not yet awakened the will, especially those who spend most of their time at Stage 0 sleep.

One of the best and most tragic examples of this stage is the life of Adolph Hitler. By all accounts of him, it seems that this man had profoundly developed his will and along with it a very distinct sense of his own identity. That will was able to withstand many forms of resistance to his chosen identity in the early years of his rise to power. But in that rise, he seemed to have an almost hypnotic effect on the minds of others. Not only was Hitler's own mind the servant of his will, but the minds of others became servants, too.

Although you are not likely to misuse Stage 3 will to the extent Hitler did, you should recognize the potentials of an unhealthy side of this developmental stage. This side of the polarity can be labeled the "egomaniac manipulator" because of the way it allows a very limited self-definition to control one's own mind, as well as those of others. This kind of *willfulness* blocks growth and makes impossible a transition to the highest stage of will.

Good will is what is required if this third stage is to be a stepping-stone to the next stage. Without an ideal of goodness coupled to empowering will, we cannot hope to grow further. If good will is extended to include the characteristic of humility, then you have the key to the healthy side of will at this stage. In other words, if you adopt a humble attitude of *willingness* instead of willfulness, then a movement to Stage 4 is possible.

It is our opportunity and our destiny to develop fully the empowering will at a personal level. Spiritual growth requires the complete empowerment of the individual life. Only then can we take the next and biggest step.

Stage 4: Transpersonal Will

Stage 4 is the Real Will of the soul, what might also be called the "transpersonal will." In traditional religion this has often been referred to as the will of God. The two points of view are not incompatible because at this level the individual's will has aligned itself with the will of God.

Surrender is required of you in order to move from Stage 3 to Stage 4. What must be given up is the extensive personal power created by empowering will. You must also surrender a certain sense of your own identity, which up until now has still maintained a high degree of separateness from the whole. It is not that Stage 4 makes you return to the oceanic feeling of oneness, which you had as an infant. It is not a loss of unique individuality. Instead, it is a surrender in which your old, mistaken notion of personal identity dies and what is resurrected is your authentic identity – your individuality. That individuality knows itself to be itself (i.e., full self-reflection) and simultaneously knows itself as one with the universe.

A subtle point is often misunderstood about surrender, death, and rebirth. The personality-self is relieved to hear that in moving from Stage 3 to Stage 4, unique personhood is not destroyed. But the personality-self assumes mistakenly that *it* shall be the identity that stays most important. To the contrary, the personality loses its primary place. What is awakened is something resembling the personality in that it knows its own distinct nature. However, this something new – this individuality in its full flower – is a quite different way of the soul experiencing itself and the universe around it.

How, then, are you to understand the experience of will at the fourth level? What would it feel like? P.D. Ouspensky put it this way:

Real Will is like suddenly seeing the solution to a mathematics problem. No doubt, we have all had the experience of working intently on some abstract issue which we knew had an answer but it seemed to elude us. Then, there may have come that instant in which we suddenly recognized the solution. The *feeling* of Real Will is much like that feeling associated with finding an answer which works.

This analogy is an especially effective one because it reminds us that the universe is orderly. The mathematician trusts that the array of scattered observations can be combined into some formula because he or she knows the universe is lawful. In the same way, we struggle with the scattered challenges and difficulties of our lives. Real Will is the recognition of creative possibilities for responding to those problems.

The Real Will or transpersonal will is that which reveals solutions. It does so by uniting the influences of life in order to create something new. The content of revelation from your transpersonal will is usually a surprise to you; its solution comes as something not considered by your personality-self. Often it is even rejected at first by your personality because of its unexpected or foreign quality. But it is this feature of "new possibilities" offered by Real Will which gives it a power to transform you far beyond the influences of Stage 3 will. *The answers and solutions proposed by empowering will are usually an extension of the personality we already are; transpersonal will reveals to us the invitation to be something more.*

We might well ask, " Why not go *directly* to Stage 4 will?' In other words, why don't we begin our efforts to awaken the will by merely inviting God's will to work through us? In fact, we can but only because it is possible to work on developing slowly all four stages simultaneously. However, this does not mean we can bypass the first three stages. Before we concern ourselves with ultimate surrender, let us be sure that we have something of substance that we are offering up. Jung worked with his patients to develop a strong sense of individual nature (ego) before moving in the individuation process to transpersonal development. Assagioli's system teaches personal psychosynthesis before spiritual psychosynthesis.

The development of the first three stages is crucial because those levels of will allow us to function in the physical plane. When we have moments in which transpersonal will awakens, the accompanying revelation will always require an application. The Real Will reveals solutions, but then the solutions must be lived in three-dimensional expression. If we have not worked to develop negating will and skillful will, as well as empowering will, then the insights, solutions, and possibilities uncovered by transpersonal will shall not truly benefit us. It is an irony of the spiritual path. We must work hard to achieve something and then be prepared to surrender it. Many times it will be given back to us, but always we must be ready to surrender it again.

Only by letting go and surrendering can you experience the highest level of will. But in what specific ways might you expect to encounter it? To what degree might you have already had small tastes of how it works?

The greatest example of surrender and transpersonal will is something you probably aren't ready for. It is Jesus' willingness to give up His personal powers and His personal desires. The scene in the Garden of Gethsemane is a lesson about letting go and being willing to follow God's plan. But even though you may not be ready for that kind of surrender, in smaller ways you have seen how it works.

Remember a day when you wanted things to go a certain way and worked hard to make it happen. Maybe it was a family reunion at your home, an important job interview, or a special vacation trip. There may have come a point where you knew that you had done all you could possibly do and now it was time just to let go. With that surrender there may have come a feeling of peace, and then some unexpected things happened. You may have seen events work out much better than you could ever have made them happen.

Or, you may have had this sort of experience with transpersonal will: a healing breakthrough in a difficult interpersonal relationship. You may have thought long and hard about how to act with this difficult person. You probably tried everything you knew how to do. Perhaps there were some improvements, but a real change seemed beyond your ability. But knowing you had done your best, you let go – you turned the problem over to something Higher. And then – like grace – it happened. Maybe you woke up one morning *knowing* what was needed. You hadn't arrived at this solution by logic. It was a gift: it was now a Higher Will directing you.

Practical Examples of Applying the Stages of Will Development

There are countless ways in which these stages play themselves out in our lives, especially when we are truly willing to change and consciously embark on a commitment to personal transformation. Let's consider just three illustrations.

Meditation. This spiritual discipline was already a focus for an entire chapter in this book. Imagine the following steps you might go through in order to have a deep meditation experience, culminating in Stage 4 in which you make a conscious connection with Higher Will.

When you first sit down to meditate, your will is probably still at Stage 0. When you close your eyes, the tendency is for your mind to flit from one thought to another. You are caught up in the worries and frustrations of the day. But through an act of will you begin to focus your attention. You use Stage 1 will to say "no" to those distracting thoughts and you make the effort to keep all of your attention on the mantra or affirmation of your choice. The use of this type of will is effective, up to a point. It can move you to a deep level of concentration, but far more is required if you are to meditate effectively.

Awakening the second stage of the will, you can begin using any forthcoming distractions to take you actually deeper into the spirit of affirmation. Employing skillful will, you can blend the content of the distraction with the motivation or ideal of the affirmation. For example, suppose that your affirmation, "Let me be a channel of blessing to others." When a distracting thought arises about your father-in-law, there is an option other than using the negating will to force the distraction aside. Instead, you can use the thought of this person to remind you of a place in your life where the ideal of loving service could be applied. You might even take a moment to feel the channeling of blessings to your father-in-law. In so doing, you may experience deeper attunement.

Continuing this process, you come to a point in meditation where your mind begins to get still. Instead of the recurring parade of images and memories surfacing from your unconscious, there is stillness. Your mind has become the servant of your will. Will at the third stage has emerged. In this personally empowering state, much is possible in meditation. You feel re-energized and at the same time profoundly relaxed and at peace. However, this is the danger zone of meditation. In her classic book on meditative and mystical states entitled *Mysticism,* Evelyn Underhill describes this state of meditation as "The Quiet." She says that it tempts the meditator to believe that he or she has now arrived. The sense of personal expansiveness and personal empowerment is dangerous if you forget that there is yet a further step: one that requires letting go.

The highest state of meditation is one in which the Real Will takes over. Here there can be a revelation of the purposes and insights of the soul. Ultimately meditation is surrender. In the end you can do nothing to *make* something happen, even with the considerable powers of Stage 3 will. There must come the surrender and the trust which allows a rebirth of your sense of identity.

Healing. The process of healing also demonstrates the developmental stages of will, particularly if healing is considered at the deepest levels of the soul and not alone the treatment of physical symptoms. As helpful a role as meditation, massage, or surgery may play, real healing must include a change in consciousness – otherwise new symptoms are likely to emerge in the future.

When you are sick, you are to some extent "asleep" in old, familiar patterns which control your thinking, feeling, acting, and even body functioning. Whether the situation is chronic headaches or cancer, there is an aspect of the will that is at Stage 0 when illness occurs. Of course, a person sick with headaches, cancer, or any other illness may have a strong, well-functioning will in some (even many) areas of life. However, the aspects of living which have produced the illness are controlled by forces which are not being directed by the will. Illness is "sleep"; dis-ease is unconsciousness (even though you may be painfully conscious of the symptoms).

Healing *begins* with a Stage 1 awakening of will in those areas, which have been producing an imbalanced condition. It starts with being able to say "no." Negation could take the form of saying "no" to a self-image of being victimized by the illness. Or, it could be rejection of one's self-images as the sickly one. In other cases, Stage 1 will is necessary in order to start saying "no" to certain thought patterns, behavior, or dietary habits which have maintained the illness.

However, healing must go deeper. Next, you are challenged to awaken Stage 2 will in these areas of life. This may mean skillfully balancing the inner and outer demands of life to make healing possible. It may mean embracing the illness itself and listening to it. Only when you reach Stage 2 will can you actually accept an illness and let it be your teacher. The symptoms of pain can often be a message – to the conscious mind or the soul itself – and the removal of symptoms may come only after the lesson has been appreciated and skillfully integrated into living.

With Stage 3 will it becomes possible for you actually to build a new body. As mind obeys the guiding direction of will and initiates new patterns of thought and emotion, then a new way of body functioning emerges. For example, biofeedback research has shown that with the will you can control and reprogram processes previously thought to be under the exclusive domain of the unconscious mind and autonomic nervous system (e.g., blood pressure, skin temperature, heart rate). But even biofeedback (i.e., "the voluntary control of internal states," as it is technically called) has its limitation. The willful removal of certain painful conditions may not amount to a real healing if the deeper cause of the illness is not dealt with. Stage 3 will may permit you to replace dysfunctional or sick aspects of your body with healthy ones, but if a healing in consciousness has not occurred, then different painful symptoms are likely to emerge.

Transpersonal will is required for the deepest level of the healing of any disease or illness. There is always an element of inexplicable grace to real healing. The progress that can be made in the healing *process* is, no doubt, important. The "will to health" unfolds as you move through States 1, 2, and 3. However, at some point you must be able to surrender and experience the Real Will of your individuality. It knows the deepest solution to your sickness. At Stage 4 you can find in its fullness the role of will in healing.

Changing habit patterns. Another practical example of the progressive stages of will development comes whenever you try to change some troublesome habit in your personality. To illustrate this, consider the example of Terry, a single, 29-year-old office manager. She has the bothersome habit of losing her temper in a wide variety of interpersonal relations – at the job, with family or friends, with herself, etc. Whenever her mechanical, automatic habit of temper flare-ups is controlling her, then she is at Stage 0 will in this part of her life.

The first stage in healing this tendency is for her to learn that she can say "no" to the compulsion to blow her stack. As she slowly begins to experience that she has an identity other than the "hot-head," then she is making constructive progress, using her will to change this habit. However, to stop with Stage 1 would mean to settle for repression of her anger, a situation which cannot have long-term benefits. Simply repressed for an indefinite period, that anger would begin to pop up elsewhere in her life, most likely as physical illness.

To progress on to Stage 2, Terry can use her will to deal with her anger more skillfully. She might do it in at least two ways. First, she can re-embrace her anger and love it. She can recognize that there is something good in her anger, even if its way of expression hasn't been very constructive. Rather then seeing her anger as an irredeemable fault, she may start seeing its good side and skillfully find new ways of using its energy and determination. Second, her Stage 2 will can allow her to start seeing in a new way the people who make her angry. This level of will may allow Terry to perceive the faults and shortcomings of others in such a fashion that she recognizes the seed or essence of something good, even in the things that used to make her explode.

The changing of this pattern can proceed further under the direction of Stage 3 will. Now Terry can use her will to start building new patterns of thought and feeling toward those who used to make her automatically so angry. Here she is not merely finding different ways to cope with or *channel* anger – she is directing her mind with her will to create new attitudes and feelings.

The temptation is to see this third stage of will awakening as the final development that Terry can make in changing this habit. By mastering Stage 3 will, she experiences a great sense of empowerment and knows that she can create whatever kinds of attitudes and feelings she wants to have toward people. Yet a more complete transformation of her problem is possible. If she listens for the promptings of Stage 4 will, she can discover a profoundly wise source of guidance, which can direct the shaping of the very *best* ways of seeing and responding to people in her life. This transpersonal will can provide the *optimal solution* to every interpersonal challenge she will face, often guiding her responses in ways that never would have occurred to her personality.

This illustration, as well as the previous ones concerning healing and meditation, are meant only as examples. There are many other situations in which you can experience this kind of sequential awakening of your will and undergo transformational change. No doubt you are at different stages with different relationships and issues. The first key for each area is to recognize the level of will development at which you currently live. Progress begins at that point. Once you recognize your current developmental level with a particular problem, then what can you do to move ahead?

The second key answers that question. Remember that most often you *cannot force* the progression. Even though you might want to set a goal to be at Stage 4 with a particular problem by next week, don't do it. Any kind of impatience only makes it more likely you shall revert to a lower stage of will in that area of life.

Because of your unique background as a soul, there is a specialized timing to how quickly you can proceed with will development in each challenging circumstance. In one relationship, you may be able to make rapid progress; in another, it may take months or years to gain mastery of the next stage. But no matter what the timing, you can maintain a patient, persistent willingness to change and take the next step on your journey of personal transformation.

Chapter 8

Methods of Awakening Your Will

A willingness to change means having a healthy will to activate the transformation process and keep it going. In the previous three chapters we have explored many aspects of free will and the role it can play in our lives. This final chapter makes the topic even more practical – exploring direct exercises and methods that can be used to awaken and strengthen this crucial power within the soul.

In a sense this chapter is about will training, but we need to be careful how we use that phrase. Is it even possible to train and develop your will? Some people say that the very phrase "will training" is circular reasoning. They point out that to awaken and develop the will by conscious effort is impossible, since the very activity presupposes that the will is already awake and able to direct the effort. This argument suggests that will training is like trying to "pull yourself up by your own boot straps" because it asks an undeveloped will to supervise its own training.

Such a pessimistic viewpoint is not a new one. It has been offered whenever human growth and development is proposed. For example, there is the riddle "Can people teach themselves?" – that is, can ignorance move toward understanding, or does learning always require a teacher who already knows? Or, put at a more profound level, "Can the unenlightened mind do anything on its own to move toward spiritual awakening, or does enlightenment always require a guru?"

This sort of philosophical question is not easily answered, but in this chapter let's at least explore at a very pragmatic level the ways that you might experience your will becoming more awake, available, and healthy. This chapter consists of ten training exercises which may help you gain a conscious, balanced relationship with your will. Undoubtedly some of the exercises are likely to seem more pertinent to you than others, and some may give you better results when applied. Approach this program as if it were a menu from which you can select and experiment.

Each one of these training strategies requires that some measure of will already be present in order to work with it. If you are "asleep," then it may never occur to you to focus attention on one of the exercises. However, in a moment in which your will is at least awakened to Stage 1 (as we called it in Chapter 7), you can focus attention and effort sufficiently to try an exercise.

Training Exercise #1: Small Group Work

Many great spiritual teachers, including Jesus and the Buddha, have worked with a small group. It is a potent vehicle for the seeker to change and grow spiritually. More specifically, there is something about a like-minded small group which facilitates the personal awakening of the will. There is a special quality found within a group *if* it has a common ideal of spiritual development. G. I. Gurdjieff (as well as his protégés such as P.D. Ouspensky and Maurice Nicoll) understood the power of a small group and often conducted that work in a group setting. In fact, much of the last fifteen years of Gurdjieff's life were spent in international travel, which included setting up groups to work with his system. In a parallel fashion, Rudolf Steiner (whose soul journey model we explored in Chapter 1) delivered a large portion of his teachings to small groups of his followers in various European cities.

What is it, then, about a small group that makes it such a special format? One possibility is that the group begins to forge a kind of "group consciousness." It acts like a field in which the personal unfoldment of each individual happens best. That field includes the features of a collective will or "pooled" will, from which each individual is able to draw in order to make choices and changes which might otherwise be much harder to accomplish alone.

The purpose is not to make the individual seeker dependent on the group. The "pooled" will is not meant to be more powerful than the individual's own awakening will, but rather a servant and helper to each individual. This is a critical distinction because groups can tragically turn into cults. The key rests with the purpose of the group. If its mission is to help each individual to flower in his or her own unique way, then a small group can be a powerful assistance for awakening and balancing the will. If the group honors the essential freedom of choice of each member, then it can be a safe method to enhance will development.

Keeping the guidelines in mind, you may want to experiment with this approach. Try a regular group activity which works with some system for spiritual growth. The system may or may not directly involve a discussion of the will itself, but it should be one which stresses personal application and responsibility. Every group is different because of the unique chemistry created by the participants. But if you can find a group which feels right to you, it may be one of the very best strategies for strengthening your will.

Training Exercise #2: Self-Observation

Learn to "stand aside and watch yourself go by." As an exercise in will, step outside yourself and observe your own thoughts, emotions, and deeds. The goal is an objective point of view. In other words, the point of this technique is *not* to be narcissistic or preoccupied with yourself. Instead, this exercise requires you to use your will to disengage your full identity momentarily from the strong habits, which usually control your thinking, feeling, and acting.

In using this technique, you do not stop your inner and outer reactions to life, but instead merely observe them in an objective way. One part of you continues without resistance in habit patterns, while another part of you disengages or dis-identifies long enough to observe the habit *as it is happening.* Only through exercising your will can such a technique be accomplished.

To illustrate how the technique might work, suppose that you have made a hurried stop-over at the bank during your lunch hour. Standing in line waiting for a teller is taking far longer than expected and you are going to be late getting back to the office. All kinds of automatic, habitual reactions arise quite predictably. They come from the part of you which has no free will and operates like a machine. Frustration, anger, worry, a churning stomach, restlessly moving around in line – all these may occur. If there is any hope for your will to alter some day those old, familiar reactions, it *won't* be through repression of them. Instead, it can start from the simple yet subtle technique of "standing aside and watching yourself go by." While these reactions are taking place, you can use your will to move in consciousness so that you are able to observe objectively what is happening.

The necessary quality of this self-observation must be *loving acceptance*. It serves no useful purpose to condemn yourself or to feel guilty. But as you learn to use your will to withdraw some of your energy and identity from those automatic habits, a surprising thing occurs. It may take weeks or months of self-observation (maybe longer), but the controlling force of that habit begins to weaken. In what may have seemed like a roundabout method, your will has been used to make a change. Instead of trying to use the will to force that change, this more gentle technique produces better results.

This powerful method of self-observation is not reserved for only negative emotional states. Nearly everyone spends most of daily living in a kind of sleeping wakefulness. The most innocuous and unemotional routines of life are good candidates for self-observation. As your will becomes stronger and more fully awakened, you shall find it easier to sustain these periods of objective self-perception. What initially could be done for only seconds at a time may be maintained for several minutes. The fruits of this technique can also include important insights about yourself which give you material for the next technique.

Training Exercise #3: Disciplines Countering Your Habits

Habit is the very antithesis of authentic will. Whenever you use your will to make efforts against the grain of the familiar, then the health and strength of your will can be enhanced. Carefully selected personal disciplines or consciousness experiments are one way to do this. For an exercise to be useful here, it needs to run counter to a habit pattern. Here are some examples.

- Speak about other people only in the way you would if they were present to hear what you'd say about them.
- Smile at strangers whom you pass.

- At mealtimes eat all of one item on your plate before moving on to the next.
- Under-plan your day -- i.e., leave time and room for surprises or the unexpected.
- Use your opposite hand more often – i.e., if you are right-handed, use your left hand more often than usual.
- Go without saying "I" for a day.

There is, of course, a degree of artificiality to most such disciplines, however, these examples are not necessarily meant to become permanent features of your behavior. For instance, whereas it may be a productive will-training exercise for a right-hander to use her left hand more frequently for a day or two, it is not expected that she would try to incorporate this "going against the grain of habit" indefinitely. In a similar fashion, it is probably impractical to eliminate permanently saying "I," but it can be a valuable exercise for twenty-four hours. On the other hand, smiling more often or speaking of others with more sensitivity may be will training exercises worth incorporating as often as the discipline can be remembered.

To use this technique, you must first have observed yourself. You need to have recognized some of your strongest habits, which occur in a mechanical, will-less way. Then you can decide upon appropriate experiments for using will – small exercises, which introduce a conscious, new approach. Some of your disciplines are likely to challenge you to more loving or thoughtful behavior (e.g., smiling at strangers), although other disciplines can be value-neutral and merely challenge you to bring more consciousness to what you do (e.g., changing your style of eating from your dinner plate).

Another version of this training strategy is to do something you dislike or "isn't like you." Of course, you should always make sure that any such discipline doesn't require you to operate against your highest ideals. However, with that important criterion in mind, consider these two examples.

When you need to ask a favor of an out-of-town friend, which method is more natural to your habitual personality – write a letter, send an e-mail, or telephone? As an act of will, you might try to do the one that most prominently "goes against the grain" of your tendency.

When you sit next to someone on a bus or airplane, what seems more natural for you to do – keep quiet unless spoken to or initiate conversation? Again, a will-training exercise for you might be consciously trying out the behavior that "isn't like you."

Training Exercise #4: Loving Self-Assertion

Much has been made of self-assertion techniques in popular psychology. Interest has largely focused on training women in the skills of assertion, but the topic is relevant to male psychology as well. The question remains whether or not such training is conducive to authentic transformation and more specifically what relationship it has to the expression of a healthy will.

If the meaning of the phrase "self-assertion" is first made clear, then practicing self-assertion can be a positive step toward a healthy will. When the "self" in question refers to your essential, inner being – your individuality – then healthy will training is possible. But if the "self" refers to the old, habitual, fear-based patterns of personality, then assertion only undermines your real will by putting you further "asleep."

In a similar way, it is helpful to clarify the word "assertion." It can have connotations of aggressiveness, and this hardly leads to a healthy will. Instead, it is possible to understand assertion in terms of *affirmation.* It means the practical expressions of your will to say clearly to the world around you, "This is who I am."

There are many helpful ways to practice this kind of creative self-assertion. One is to express positive feelings. As an act of will, practice communicating good feelings. Use your will first to put aside fears that you are being corny, pushy, or prideful. Then, when it is appropriate and honest, use your will and affirm words like these:

- I really enjoy being with you.
- I feel good about what I just accomplished.
- Thanks for appreciating me.
- I really like the way you handled that.

Another kind of self-assertion skill is to set limits. In many ways this incorporates a balanced use of Stage 1 will because it requires that you say "no" to certain things. By communicating to others the parameters in which you are willing to relate to them, you affirm who you are. Of course, the examples below may not fit the limits you want to set. But as you express your *own* limits by loving self-assertion, you are using and strengthening your will. For example:

- Thanks, but I don't need any help.
- I wish that you wouldn't make commitments for me.
- I would appreciate your not smoking
- I would like to think further about that before deciding what to do.

Training Exercise #5: Stay in the Now

To train and strengthen your will, keep your attention in the now. Act in the now. It sounds simple, but most people have great difficulty doing this. Consider some of the ways in which you may try to use your will out of sync with its natural, effective place: in the present moment.

- Do you fantasize and rehearse well in advance what you are going to do and say? Do you constantly anticipate the future, dwelling on scenarios that may or may not even happen? This mistaken use of the will goes far beyond prudent thoughts or plans about the future; it exhausts your will. When you carefully observe your thought patterns, do you find anxiety-directed visualizations about the future (e.g., a showdown with the boss or a date with an idolized member of the opposite sex)? There is a great problem created by such attempts to force the future along a certain course. It is not only a waste of mental energy but, the event never turns out as anticipated. When you confront the situation as it finally manifests, it is different than expected and suddenly your will is disoriented and ineffective.
- How often do you catch yourself trying to use your will to *force* something to happen "before its time has come?" This phrase may sound poetic, but nature itself shows the deep

wisdom in "right timing." Living organisms, like the human psyche and body, are largely governed by hidden rhythms and destinies. In this case, the misuse of the will is to impose a conscious agenda on some developing process. In what ways might you find yourself doing this? Perhaps in trying to get a friend interested in changing before he or she is ready. Or, attempting to get the garden to produce ripe tomatoes a week earlier than normal. As a parent, do you push your preschool child to grow up too soon, learning to read or do arithmetic before other children? Or trying to lose 10 pounds when your body isn't ready for the discipline that may be required. The possibilities are endless, and only by careful self-observation can you see how you may be misapplying your will to force things out of their natural timing.

- Do you try to change your past? This erroneous use of will goes beyond a healthy consideration of the lessons to be learned from past experiences. Most frequently, this misapplication of will involves continually dwelling on some mistake, as if you could change what happened merely by willing it to be so. However, your capacity to make changes resides in the present moment alone. Only in the now is your will able to express its potent capabilities to direct and alter the course of life.

In a sense this particular will-training exercise is the most fundamental one. Other techniques, such as meditation, self-observation, and self-assertion, all require your attention and point of application to be *in the present moment*.

Training Exercise #6: Positive Imitation

The next four training exercises are adapted from the teachings of Rudolf Steiner, regarding the education of the will in children. The Waldorf School curriculum, founded on Steiner's philosophy, includes many principles concerning the awakening of a healthy will function. Although each of these four training strategies are most fundamentally relevant to work with children, we can infer that to some degree they can be adapted and made applicable to adult efforts to awaken and strengthen the will.

The first of the four techniques is *positive imitation*. Your will can be awakened and strengthened by observing other people who have a healthy will. In the Waldorf School setting, the example is the teacher, but as adults you must identify your "teachers" in a more informal way.

To get this started, review the seven qualities of the will outlined in Chapter 6. Who are the people in your life who do a better job than you in manifesting those qualities? Can you find more time to be with such people? Or can you at least be more attentive when you are around them as to *how* they deal with the challenges of life? These attentive efforts can show results as you learn to demonstrate your own healthy will through purposeful imitation.

Another, and more indirect, method to work with this training approach is to read and study biographical accounts of great men and women who manifested a healthy will. Some readers find that the objective, narrative approach of a biographer is most helpful in learning about the will. Others find that the subjective, personal account provided by an autobiography is more meaningful, because it provides a more direct way to experience the thinking, feeling, and willing processes of that great person.

Training Exercise #7: Building Rhythms into Life

In the Waldorf School setting, the will is educated in the context of meaningful repetition and rhythm. The child is taught the natural rhythms of living – those organic patterns found in the earth's seasons, the cycles of plant growth, and even the recurrent elements in the cycle of a single day. As adults, there is much that can still be learned by the appreciation of purposeful, conscious repetitions in life.

The will is awakened and trained through repetition in more than one way. First, there must be willed effort to maintain the pattern. For example, it takes some effort to get a positive habit started. But then, once the pattern is established, the will can, in turn, begin to draw sustenance from the rhythm itself.

This process is illustrated in the discipline of keeping a regular meditation time each day. At first it takes effort. All kinds of excuses to procrastinate or avoid keeping the appointed time arise from the mind. By acts of will the regular pattern is established. However, with the creation of such a personal rhythm, a remarkable thing begins to happen. The rhythm has a life of its own. Keeping the meditation time becomes easier, no longer requiring a struggle or undue effort. The will itself begins to be fed and strengthened by the purposeful pattern.

Consider how you might use this training exercise in your own life. First, are there ways that you could start being sensitive to the rhythms of nature? Your will can be nurtured as you consciously participate in those patterns. Perhaps it means paying attention to sunrises and sunsets. Or it might be an involvement in the seasons of nature through a backyard vegetable garden or a fruit and berry orchard.

Second, select one or two personal behaviors that can be established as personal rhythms. It may be meditation, reading, exercise, playtime with children, or any other purposeful activity that can be repeated regularly.

Training Exercise #8: Let Go of Mechanization

Society offers an incredible array of labor-saving machines. There are so many shortcuts to getting things done which are available to members of Western technological culture. The list seems endless. Each device saves you time and most significantly it saves you *effort.*

But what price do you pay for becoming more and more dependent upon machines and appliances to avoid effort? Aren't there both overt and subtle ways in which your will is undermined? A labor-saving device permits your force of will to remain inactive or even asleep. For example, excessive use of movies and television for entertainment destroys your own capacity for will-directed imagination. Why should the will be alive and playfully active with the mind, when it is possible to sit back passively and receive fascinating images?

But if you are serious about awakening and training your will, just how far should you take this? Surely deep personal transformation is not made more efficient by throwing out vacuum cleaners, electric toothbrushes, and power drills. Most likely your present way of living and your commitments don't make it possible to eliminate many labor-saving machines. But rather than just to ignore the impact they have on your will, it is still possible to design some will enhancing *experiments* which reintroduce personal effort to areas where depending on a machine is easy.

For example, suppose you enjoy music in your life. Perhaps you are the sort of person who can play one or more instruments in a marginally skillful and amateurish way. Rather than flip on the stereo or radio every time you want some music, you could periodically use your will to create your own music. Certainly it won't be of the professional caliber that you would hear otherwise, but you're likely to discover a vast *qualitative* difference in your experience of music when your will is involved.

Or, consider the short trips which you make by automobile, which could have been accomplished by walking or biking. It may take some planning because of the longer time involved, but it can reawaken you to the meaning of physical distance (something easily lost by the hypnotic effect of modern auto and jet travel).

If you are a public speaker, occasionally try to make your presentation without an amplification system. Obviously there are settings which make this impossible. In some auditoriums it would mean that many people just wouldn't hear your unaided voice. But aren't there times when you use electronic amplification out of habit or because you won't have to make as concerted an effort to reach people with your voice? What you are likely to discover is that your voice, directly received by listeners without the intervention of a mechanical device, creates a different kind of relationship between you and your audience. At least in part, this is the product of your will as a more active force in the relationship.

Structure your experimental disciplines as you did in Training Exercise #3 (i.e., "Disciplines Countering Your Habits"). Your efforts to do something without a labor-saving machine may be only for a short period of time. For example, use a manual instead of electric can opener for a week. Or your experiment may take the form of commitment. For example, once each week replace one short automobile trip with a walk; or write one letter a week when you would usually have made a long distance phone call instead.

It is not the purpose of this training exercise to alienate you from the modern world. No doubt, effort-saving machines will continue to be a large part of your life. But taking them for granted and ignoring the indirect influence they have on will is inadvisable. Merely the *occasional* reliance upon your own efforts instead of a machine's can help keep your will alert. In so doing, your will is available to use creatively the time that the machines free up for you.

Training Exercise #9: Moving the Limbs of the Body Purposefully

In Rudolf Steiner's system of thought, there are three key functions: thinking, feeling, and willing. In correlating these three with the parts of the physical body, the following associations are made:

- Thinking especially engages the head and brain;
- Feeling especially engages the trunk and internal organs;
- Willing especially engages the limbs.

In the Waldorf Schools, the child is given will-educating activities which purposefully involve movement of the arms and legs. Because the associations described above continue throughout human life, this training strategy is probably pertinent to adult will training as well.

As part of your personal program to awaken your will further, you may wish to select some kind of activity that involves purposeful body movements. For some people, will training is achieved through hatha yoga practice or t'ai chi exercises. For others, it can happen through a regular program of running, walking, or biking. For those who have access to skilled teachers of Gurdjieff's system, there is training in his elaborate "movements" which require an awakening of the will forces. In a similar fashion, there are schools which offer instruction in Steiner's eurythmy, body movements which make visible the realms of music and voice.

In a sense, this training exercise is the most straightforward of the twelve presented in this chapter. Depending on what approach you choose, varying amounts of dedication are required, but it is easy to see how body movements require the use of will.

Training Exercise #10: Set a Reachable Goal Daily

The final will-enhancement method is based on the adage that says, "Nothing succeeds like success." Nothing gives you a clearer, stronger sense of your will than to use it successfully. But a major obstacle you may face in training your will is the temptation to force the accomplishment of goals too quickly – to try to change something with your will which for the moment is really beyond your reach.

Imagine a high jumper who wishes she could clear a height of six feet. She knows from experience that she can regularly clear five feet, but the six-foot level seems far beyond her current abilities – only a wish, a dream. But she is determined to make this change in her abilities. She intends to use her will and to accomplish her goal.

How then should she proceed? One option is for her to set the high jump bar at six feet every day in her practice sessions and continually try to clear it. She is going to have continual failures, but she hopes that eventually she might succeed.

Another option is to set little goals that progressively move her toward her ultimate goal. First, she would set the high jump bar at five feet one inch. She would work to clear that height consistently and, in so doing, build up her feeling of success and confidence. Inch by inch she would work her way up. Each new goal would be a small step requiring her will to call forth just a little more strength and skill. These small, reachable goals would provide her with feelings of confidence and success, which are likely to lead to her larger goal.

The analogy is pertinent to your own life. Create for yourself the daily experience of successfully using your will. Each night before you go to bed or first thing in the morning, set a reachable goal. It is something that requires a little effort – a reasonable application of your will – but it is certainly within your capability to do it. Probably the goal is usually going to be something new each day, but sometimes it will seem right to repeat one from a previous day. They may lead progressively toward a more ambitious goal, or they may be diverse and each day address something different in your life. Here are some of my examples, although you should make up your own list:

- Compliment my wife at least once.
- Do five minutes of calisthenics before breakfast.
- Read five pages in the book I've been trying to get through.
- Write one letter to a friend.
- Greet one stranger I pass on the sidewalk.

Remember, create just one reachable goal each day. Then, get it done. Experience a success with your will. Get to know that feeling of accomplishment. These small, daily successes build on each other and create greater confidence for you. They lead to a healthier, stronger will.

Summary

Design a will-training program for yourself, using as many of these ten exercises as you like. They can be done in any order, and you may be able to work on several of them during the same period of time. You are encouraged to design some kind of chart to keep track of your commitments and results with specific exercises.

And as you practice these exercises and watch your will become stronger, it makes it more and more likely that your "willingness to change" will be translated into authentic "personal transformation."

Epilogue

This book aspires to be a practical and inspirational handbook for people in life transition. Whenever circumstances and demands throw your life into upset, you're faced with a challenge – to resist what's happening *or* to choose to embrace the forces of change. Hopefully, from the chapters of this book you have begun to discover how to use the momentum of change to bring more meaning and purpose into your life. The goal has been to help you understand how a painful, disorienting "growing edge" is part of the process by which a new self can emerge.

Returning to one of the central points of the first chapter: there are two different kinds of change. One is superficial "self-improvement," and it certainly has its place. The other is deep "personal transformation," and it's to that kind of change that this book invites you. As you have moved through its chapters, hopefully you have found yourself taken more fully into the process of personal transformation – the re-creation of who you are and the way you experience the world around you. In response to the demands of change in your life, the principles and methods described in this book are intended to help you move from boredom, frustration, and "willfulness" into an accepting, creative "willingness" to live as a whole person.

However, you need more than just a book. Reading can be a powerful way to support your change process, but *personal contact is an indispensable part of the equation, too.* That "personal contact" needs to be with others who are also committed to transformative change. To that end, since the year 2000 a substantial portion of my own work as an educator has been with people who are ready to work deeply on themselves. My wife, Mary Elizabeth Lynch, and I co-founded with Dr. Rudolf Wilhelm in that year the Personal Transformation and Courage Institute. We have developed an array of courses that both challenge *and* support seekers to work with their growing edges for change.

Usually presented as three-day intensives with ten to twenty participants, these courses are a powerful way to experience directly the principles of transformation outlined in this book. Among the course themes are topics that have been frequently addressed in these chapters:

- Vision and Courage
- Healing the Courageous Heart
- Ideals, Intuition, and Guidance

Our courses are offered through several organizations in their settings *and* through settings that we arrange independently. They take place in many cities across the United States, and details can be found at our web site – transformationandcourage.org – which includes a schedule and a photo essay of what it's like to take part in one of these courses.

But even if a course like this is not possible for you, it's important nevertheless to find your "allies" and support people. The journey of personal transformation need not be undertaken alone. The power of participating in like-minded, supportive groups enhances your personal work and moves you more quickly through the transformation process.

The hope and beauty of this work comes from what happens as you make these deep changes. Your talents are liberated in order to starting living more fully what you are really here to do in the world.

ABOUT THE AUTHOR

Mark Thurston, Ph.D. is an educator, psychologist, and author of eighteen books about practical spirituality. His previous publications include *Edgar Cayce's Predictions For The 21st Century*, *The Essential Edgar Cayce*, *Discovering Your Soul's Purpose*, *Dreams: Tonight's Answers for Tomorrow's Questions*, and *Synchronicity As Spiritual Guidance.* He is also co-author of two highly practical guidebooks to personal change: *The Edgar Cayce Handbook for Creating Your Future* (with Christopher Fazel) and *Twelve Positive Habits of Spiritually Centered People* (with his daughter, Sarah Thurston).

Dr. Thurston currently serves as a faculty member in transpersonal psychology and Director of Academic Affairs for Atlantic University in Virginia Beach, Virginia. His courses and classes include a training program designed to equip people to serve as spiritual mentors.

In 1998 he was executive producer and on-air host of *The New Millennium*, a series of twenty-six television programs produced at WHRO, the PBS affiliate for the Norfolk and Virginia Beach, Virginia area. Those shows, were aired for two years on The Wisdom Channel.

Dr. Thurston and his wife Mary Elizabeth Lynch, J.D., are two of the three co-founders of the Personal Transformation and Courage Institute, a non-profit educational organization offering intensive courses in life purpose and transformational healing. He can be contacted at: www.transformationandcourage.org.

Other Books by Mark Thurston

Edgar Cayce's Predictions For The 21st Century

The Essential Edgar Cayce

Twelve Positive Habits of Spiritually Centered People (co-author)

Edgar Cayce's Guide to Spirituality for Busy People

Synchronicity as Spiritual Guidance

The Edgar Cayce Handbook for Creating Your Future (co-author)

Soul-Purpose: Discovering and Fulfilling Your Destiny

Dreams: Tonight's Answers for Tomorrow's Questions

Paradox of Free Will

The Inner Power of Silence

Discovering Your Soul's Purpose

How to Interpret Your Dreams

Face to Face (co-author)

Understand and Develop Your ESP

Experiments in Practical Spirituality

Experiments in a Search for God

Meditation and the Mind of Mind (co-author)

Printed in the United States
50506LVS00001B/29-42

9 781929 841264